FOTO

T:O

88

f©°

FEST

ISBN Number: 0-9619766-5-9
Libriary of Congress Catalogue Number: 97-81239

FotoFest
3400 Montrose, Suite 801
Houston, Texas 77006
713.529.9140
fax 713.529.9160
info@fotofest.org

Design: Pennebaker Design
Printing: Masterpiece Litho, Inc.

SPONSORS

The Seventh International Month of Photography
and Literacy Through Photography Program

WITHDRAWN

FOTOFEST 1997-98 FUNDERS
The Brown Foundation in honor of Carol Crow
William Stamps Farish Fund
The Cullen Foundation
Houston Endowment Inc.
The City of Houston and the Texas Commission for the Arts
    through the Cultural Arts Council and by a Regional
    Touring Grant from Harris County through the Cultural
    Arts Council
Susan Vaughan Foundation
AT&T
The Wortham Foundation
The Caddell and Chapman Foundation for the Arts
The Clayton Fund
The Favrot Fund
Harris and Eliza Kempner Fund
Sarah Campbell Blaffer Foundation
The Powell Foundation
Scurlock Foundation
Timothy B. Maher
Trust for Mutual Understanding
George and Mary Josephine Hamman Foundation
Houston Cellular
MetLife Foundation
Adolph O. Susholtz
Margaret Cullinan Wray Charitable Lead Annuity Trust
Carolyn Grant Fay
Arthur Andersen & Company
Houston Lighting & Power Company
Hobby Family Foundation
The Samuels Foundation of The Endowment Fund of the
    Jewish Community of Houston
Morgan Personette Properties
Asian Cultural Council
French Cultural and Scientific Services
Pro Helvetia, Arts Council of Switzerland
Project Row Houses

MAJOR IN-KIND CONTRIBUTORS
Continental Airlines
British Arts Council
Weingarten Realty
Fuji Photo Film USA, Inc.
Canon USA Inc.
Fuji Color Processing, Inc.
Consulate General of Peru in Houston
Consulate General of Switzerland in Houston
Consulate General of France in Houston
Minister of Foreign Relations of Peru
Embassy of Peru in Athens, Greece
Embassy of Peru in Paris, France
Foreign Ministry of Slovakia
Embassy of Slovakia, Washington, D.C.
KUHF 88.7 FM
The Houston Chronicle
Greater Houston Convention & Visitors Bureau
Houston Convention & Entertainment Facilities Department
Pennebaker Design
Houston Cellular
Downtown District
Theater District Association
Downtown Historic District
Align Solutions
Sotheby's Inc.
The Wyndham Warwick
Creative Marketing/CMS
British Airways
Air France
Eatzi's Market and Bakery
Neosoft
Sicardi-Sanders Gallery
Gruppo Riello Spa

SPONSORS

CO-SPONSORSHIPS, EXHIBITS

Vine Street Studios
Winter Street Art Center
Wagon Works Building
Purse Building Studios
Erie City Ironworks
Sweeney, Coombs & Fredericks Building
Shoe Market Building
One Allen Center
NationsBank Center
Transco Tower
Palace Cafe and Hogg Grill
Solero
Market Square Bar and Grill
Houston Community College Central
Rice University Gallery
Rice Media Center
Project Row Houses
The Community Artists Collective
Art League of Houston
William Street Gallery
Treebeards

AUCTION SPONSORS

Walter and Karen Bering
Alan and Helen Buckwalter
Michael A. Caddell and Cynthia B. Chapman
Bob and Mary Kay Casey
Mavis and Wendy Kelsey
James C. Kempner
Lynn Lasher and Courtney Lanier
James Edward Maloney and Beverly Ann Young
William N. and Lisa Mathis
Northern Trust Bank
Mary Porter
Bonnie Rubey
Mike and Anita Stude
Terry and Alice Thomas
Texas Commerce Bank–Chase
El Matha Wilder

AUCTION CONTRIBUTORS

Sotheby's, New York
The Houston Chronicle
tony's...at home
Absolut Vodka
Mamba Beer
Fixtures International
Mission Burritos

BOARD OF DIRECTORS

Fred Baldwin, *President*
Michael A. Caddell, *Board Secretary*
Mary Kay Casey, *Board Chairperson*
Paul B. Clemenceau
Herman E. Detering, III
Richard Duncan
Martin Feinberg
Daphne Wood Gawthrop
Cab Gilbreath
Carola Herrin
Mavis Kelsey
James C. Kempner
Melanie Lawson
James Edward Maloney
William N. Mathis
John E. (Sandy) Parkerson
R. Stan Pieringer
Anne W. Tucker
Wendy Watriss, *Artistic Director*
El Matha Wilder

Frederick Baldwin and Wendy Watriss
Artistic Direction and General Management

STAFF

Ellen Ray, *Executive Director*
David F. Brown, Director, *Literacy Through Photography*
Diane Barber, *Exhibitions/Publications Coordinator*

CONSULTANTS

Martha Skow, *Coordinator, International Meeting Place and Auction*
Marta Sánchez Philippe, *Coordinator, International Projects*
Leigh Martinez, *Exhibitions/Publications Coordinator*
Christine Rosales, *Public Relations and Administrative Assistant*
Susan Elmore, Elmore Public Relations
Pennebaker Design, *Graphic Design*
Jim Kanan, Kanan Construction, *Festival Production*
Keith Hollingsworth, *Matting/Framing*
Becky Kightlinger, Art Secure, *Exhibit Installation*
Bill Kelly, *Exhibit Installation*
Jim Tebault, *Exhibit Graphics*
Mariko Kimura, Forrest Ben Thomas, *Exhibit Signage*
Ruth Antonius, World Travel & Cruises, *Travel Coordinator*
Bruce Leutwyler & Andrew Bartelt, Zentek Computer
Jeff Johnson and Ken Darnell, Brilliant Computers
Philippe Paravicini, *Web Site Design*
Phil Davis, *Lighting*

SPECIAL FESTIVAL PROGRAMS

Keith Krumweide, *Streetscape Design*
Dung Ngo, *Streetscape Project*
Production Art, *Projections*
Andy DiRaddo, LD Systems, *Lighting*

CATALOGUE

Wendy Watriss
Leslie Carolyn Johnson, *Catalogue Coordinator*
Michelle Nichols, *Copy Editor*
Marta Sanchez Philippe, *Copy Editor*
David Lerch, Pennebaker Design, *Art Director/Designer*
Rochelle Freedman, Pennebaker Design, *Project Manager*
Sandy Mooneyham, *Production Artist*
Haesun Kim Lerch, Pennebaker Design, *Designer*
Masterpiece Litho Inc., *Printing*
Diane Barber, *Text and Image Coordinator for Gallery Exhibits*
Leigh Martinez, *Text and Image Coordinator for Events*

SPECIAL ACKNOWLEDGMENT FROM THE EXECUTIVE DIRECTOR

A number of individuals worked hard to make my first year at FotoFest an exciting and rewarding one. My special thanks to FotoFest's Board of Directors for their assistance and support, particularly Mary Kay Casey, James E. Maloney, Daphne Gawthrop, and Sandy Parkerson. Susan Garwood and Claire Squibb were invaluable to me; both have terrific insight and are tireless in their enthusiasm for FotoFest. Susan Elmore, Jennifer Jones, and Rochelle Freedman helped me to keep up with the details without losing sight of the big picture — or my sense of humor!

Little would have been accomplished without FotoFest's terrific staff, particularly Leigh Martinez, whose energy and dedication to the organization made it a pleasure to come to work every day. And finally, my deepest appreciation and gratitude to Fred Baldwin and Wendy Watriss for giving me a wonderful oppor—tunity to share in their vision. Their commitment to FotoFest is both infectious and inspiring.

Ellen Ray, Executive Director

CONTENTS

DISCOVERIES AND COLLABORATIONS

FREDERICK BALDWIN
WENDY WATRISS

Houston, Johannesburg, Hanoi, Helsinki, Lima, Bratislava, Mexico City, Los Angeles, São Paulo, Florence, San Antonio, Paris, Poprad, Xalapa, New York

Festivals bring forth surprises, new discoveries, connections, and collaborations. In Europe, Latin America, and Asia, photography festivals are growing in number. They are vehicles for collective activity in cities, channels for international exchange, and avenues for the discovery of new artistic talent.

With the 1998 International Month of Photography, FotoFest again looks towards new horizons, perspectives, and ideas. In preparation for the seventh biennial festival of photography, FotoFest has represented Houston at Copenhagen 96, the European City of Culture; Fotoseptiembre and the Fifth Latin American Colloquium in Mexico City; Mois de la Photo in Paris; NAFOTO in São Paulo; the 1997 Rencontres at Arles; FotoFeis in Scotland; the Month of Photography in Bratislava; and Photo98 in York, England. Many of the artists, curators, and participants who are part of FotoFest exhibitions, the International Meeting Place, the Fine Print Auction, and the meeting of International Festival Directors have come from these encounters and connections around the world.

Cities are catalysts and repositories for creative energy, individual and collective. In Houston, the configuration of FotoFest 98 reflects the multifaceted presence of arts activities throughout the central city. In downtown Houston and many inner-city neighborhoods, the arts are playing a central role in the revitalization of the city. Over ninety organizations in Houston's central city are collaborating in this year's festival.

In 1998, FotoFest brings new exhibitions to Houston and the United States. These exhibitions highlight not only artists who are not yet well known in this country, but also new curatorial talent from abroad. They are an outgrowth of FotoFest's international network of organizations. With two shows from Slovakia, *Altered Worlds* and *Infusion*, FotoFest builds on a longtime commitment to Central and Eastern Europe. FotoFest 98 is working with Slovak curator Lucia Benická and the House of Photography in Poprad, Slovakia to present the first group showing in the U.S. of seven contemporary Slovak photographers whose conceptual and staged photographic works are considered one of the most original movements in postmodernist European photography. The site-specific installation *Infusion* by L'ubo Stacho presents work by one of the most innovative and experimental of an older generation of Slovak artists.

In Mexico, a new generation of artists as well as photohistorians, educators, and critics is enriching the photographic arts. The Centro de la Imagen and Patricia Mendoza have not only been a central focus for young artists in Mexico City, but they also have reached out to support new initiatives around the country in Guadalajara, Hermosillo, Mérida, Xalapa, and Tijuana, among other places. To incorporate their perspectives, we asked four Mexican colleagues who know the current photography scene in Mexico to make independent selections of three to five individual artists whose work is not well known outside of Mexico but representative of an important aspect of what is happening in Mexican photography today. *Looking at the 90s (Mirando los 90s)* presents eighteen artists, most in their thirties. The four curators are José Antonio Rodríguez, critic for El Financiero; Osvaldo Sánchez, well known writer on the visual arts and recently visual arts curator for the Festival Cervantino in Guanajuato; Ana Casas, coordinator of workshops and education at Centro de la Imagen in Mexico City; and Miguel Fematt, director and cofounder of the photographic arts program at the University of Veracruz in Xalapa.

Mexico City and the Fifth Latin American Colloquium at the Centro de la Imagen were the connections to South Africa through Cuban curator Eugenio Valdés Figueroa, who worked with artists in Africa as part of the Havana Bienal and Centro Wilfredo Lam. He put FotoFest in touch with Linda Givon, director of the Goodman Gallery, considered the leading contemporary art gallery in Johannesburg. Givon, described as "an altruist who religiously nurtures the work of artists in whom she believes," enabled the show, *Installations/Five South African Artists*, to come to life.

Connections with Paris have been strong from the beginning of FotoFest in the early 1980s. The Mois de la Photo in Paris provided the link to two 1998 exhibitions: Eugène (Eugenio) Courret from Peru and Pentti Sammallahtti from Finland. The nineteenth century Peruvian portraitist first came to our attention through its presentation at the 1994 Mois de la Photo in Paris. Two Latin American historians and critics, Dr. Keith McElroy from the University of Arizona and Fernando Castro, became persuasive voices on the importance of having this master shown in the U.S. A 1996 trip to the Mois de la Photo made possible by Association Française d'Action Artistique (AFAA) and the French Consulate in Houston enabled us to put the Peruvian opportunity into motion. That trip also reconnected us with the work of a Finnish photographer, Pentti Sammallahtti, whose work we have followed since the late 1980s. A new retrospective of his work in Paris, along with the publication of his new portfolio on Russia, made it clear that Sammallahtti's work should be introduced to audiences in the U.S.

First in New York and then at the Rencontres at Arles, Martino Marangoni from the Fondazione Marangoni in Florence talked about a show of new landscape photography from Italy. Although well known in Italy and in Europe, this movement had not been shown very much in the United States. Without totally abandoning the aesthetics of formalism, these five artists challenge classical ways of looking at Italy and the post–World War II "landscape." Their work is a bridge *Between Past and Present*. It was also at Arles that we met with representatives from Magnum Photos in Paris to look at Harry Gruyeart's show. Gruyeart is one of the first photographers to move color street photography away from documentation into the realms of metaphor and symbol.

Re-Imagining Vietnam, a special collaboration with the Art Department of Houston Community College, is another link between one world and another. Positioned at the center of Vietnamese American redevelopment of Houston's midtown and a growing Asian American student body, Mike Golden of the Houston Community College Art Department was interested in having a show about Vietnam today. A visit to Hanoi in 1996 and assistance from David Thomas of the Indochina Arts Project put us in touch with a group of young U.S. photographers who have been working on very personal perspectives of the country and exchange with Vietnamese photographers. As part of the program, a Vietnamese photographer will come to Houston to be part of a panel about Vietnam today.

Another collaboration extends FotoFest's multifaceted working relationship with Project Row Houses. Sharing resources makes it possible to bring nationally known artists to Houston for a residency and extended project at Project Row Houses. Danny Tisdale, an African American artist known for his performance-related, interactive community work linking art and political issues, will be in Houston working at Project

Row Houses over a period of two months to create a special installation around issues of community change and the Third Ward.

FotoFest's second *Discoveries of the Meeting Place* show highlights ten artists whose work was discovered by a group of curators at FotoFest's 1996 portfolio review. It is an extension of what the Wall Street Journal has called "the right place at the right time" for photographers: "For many contemporary art photographers, that place and time is Houston, during FotoFest, the International Month of Photography—and more specifically... the festival's Meeting Place, where the international photographic community converges every two years to scout out new talent."

An important retrospective of Houston-based artist Frank Martin is being done by the Art League of Houston. Rice University Gallery has invited nationally known multimedia artist Gary Hill to do his first site-based work in Houston. Another multimedia artist, Stephen Marc from Chicago, will do his first Houston show at Community Artists Collective.

Museums, nonprofit arts spaces, and commercial galleries are presenting an unusually broad spectrum of work. Among their exhibits are: DiverseWorks Artspace's inaugural presentation of photojournalism from Ciudad Juárez; Houston Center for Photography's mixed media work of U.S. artists George Peters, Melanie Walker, and Carlos Diaz; the Orange Show's history of art cars; the presentation of German artist Kai-Olaf Hesse at the Goethe Institute; the Contemporary Arts Museum's focus on five contemporary Gulf Coast artists; and the Museum of Fine Arts' *Years Ending in Nine* from the permanent collection. Among the commercial galleries, there are several firsts: Sicardi Sanders Gallery's retrospective of Brazilian avant-garde artist Gerardo de Barros; Robert McClain's show of Nobuyoshi Araki; and Pampa Risso-Patrón's exhibition of Joaquim Paiva's Brazilian collection at Barbara Davis Gallery at Pennzoil Place.

National artists are being shown by Devon Borden and Hiram Butler Gallery (James Turrell), Lawing Gallery (Uta Barth), New Gallery (David Levinthal), and John Cleary Gallery (Paul Caponigro). Among fifty-five Houston-area artists being shown are MANUAL (Moody Gallery), Keith Carter (McMurtrey Gallery and Galveston Arts Center), Kimberly Gremillion (Parkerson Gallery), Casey Williams (Barbara Davis Gallery), John Herrin and Claire Chauvin (Weekend Gallery), and Dorinth Dougherty (James Gallery).

In addition to the exhibitions, FotoFest 98 is experimenting with two other ways of making the festival interact with the city and support efforts to promote public use of the downtown area and the image of downtown as a place where things are happening. We have worked with Keith Krumweide and Dung Ngo of Rice University School of Architecture, to use the sidewalks and existing public spaces and structures to design a marking system, *Detour Streetscape,* that will create public pathways between the Theater District and Market Square Historic District.

To emphasize the sense of "happening" and the arts as catalyst for the nontraditional use of urban spaces, we have also commissioned Johannes Birringer and artists with a new company, AlienNation, to create a performance series, *Parachute,* in the area of downtown exhibition sites.

Alongside these programs and the exhibitions, Fotofest's International Meeting Place will bring together nearly 400 international curators, editors, dealers, and photographers for eight days of portfolio reviews. FotoFest's third Fine Print Auction will offer collectors work from the U.S., Europe, Latin America, and Asia.

A first for FotoFest 98 is the International Festival Directors Meeting. The idea originated at FotoFest in 1994 and, since then, an informal group has met at photography festivals and events in Denmark, Mexico, Brazil, and Scotland.

These earlier meetings took place at sites that became more exotic with each occasion: a private estate on the coast of Denmark; Francisco Toledo's new photography center in Oaxaca; a ranch near São Paulo; and finally, a windswept castle in Scotland, complete with ancestral portraits, ghosts, and haggis.

Since the purpose of these meetings is to find ways for photography festivals and events to cooperate and to create closer ties between culturally diverse organizations, we have decided to substitute "new world technology" for old world charm. There will be hands-on training with electronic technology aimed at furthering intergroup communication and collaboration. Toward this end, Ray deMoulin, former manager of Eastman Kodak's Professional Division and current head of an organization that can be characterized as a web-site encyclopedia of photo-related information, will provide hands-on instruction with new photography techniques and create a special web-site for directors of photography festivals and events. The FotoFest International Festival Directors Meeting combines practicality, technology, and, of course, Texas hospitality. With invitees from thirty countries, it is yet another example of the international network of collaborations.

1997-98 brought a number of new developments for FotoFest. The Literacy Through Photography (LTP) program started a charter school, the Kaleidoscope School, at Cunningham Elementary School in Houston to develop a demonstration and teacher training site for FotoFest's ongoing education program. The long-awaited FotoFest book, *Image and Memory, Photography from Latin America 1866-1994*, was published by the University of Texas Press in January 1998. The FotoFest 1996 exhibition of Susan Meiselas' book project, *Kurdistan, In The Shadow of History*, opened a year-long series of photography events in England in January 1998. The show was a coproduction of FotoFest and the Menil Collection. Another 1996 exhibition, *Mountain Folks of Yunan* by Chinese photo-grapher Wu Jialin, was featured at Maison de la Chine in Paris and the photography festival in Herte, Germany. Wu Jialin was also the recipient of awards from Leica Camera and the Mother Jones Foundation. The 1994 FotoFest exhibition, *American Voices, Latino Photographers in the U.S.*, had a successful five-month run at the Smithsonian Institution International Gallery in Washington during 1997 and is being converted to a national traveling show by the Smithsonian Institution Traveling Exhibition Services (SITES), with a book to be published by the Smithsonian Institution Press.

SPECIAL ACKNOWLEDGMENTS

This year, we have been graced by a new Executive Director, Ellen Ray, who started work with FotoFest a year ago. Her leadership, energy, and intelligence have been invaluable to the management of FotoFest and the production of the 1998 festival.

The FotoFest Board of Directors has contributed in many ways to FotoFest successes this year. As Board Chairperson, Mary Kay Casey has come through over and over again on behalf of FotoFest. Jim Maloney, Michael Caddell, Sandy Parkerson, Anne Tucker, Will Mathis, Jim Kempner, Carola Herrin, and El Matha Wilder have provided FotoFest with strong programmatic support. Claire Squibb's assistance has been enormously important to many aspects of FotoFest.

FotoFest's continuing involvement with downtown and the popular use of new spaces in the Warehouse Districts and the Theater District/Market Square/Main Street areas would not be possible without the generosity and vision of many property owners and developers. Fletcher Thorne-Thomson's Vine Street Studios across Main Street from the University of Houston-Downtown and Harvey Seigle's Winter Street Art Center off Washington Avenue west of downtown provided FotoFest 1998 with two of its most important exhibition sites. Also in the Commerce Street and

NoHo Warehouse areas, we want to thank Jack and Stephanie Stenner at Purse Building Studios, Roy Murray and Nancy Worthington at the Wagon Works Building on Crawford, and Kathy Nelson at Erie City Ironworks. In the Market Square/Theater District area, we are particularly grateful for the support of Jamie Mize and Dan Tidwell of Treebeards, John Tsertos at QRT Management, Cinda Ward of the Palace Cafe, Sharon Haynes of Solero, and Kent Marshall of the Market Square Bar and Grill.

The energy and enthusiasm of many people involved with downtown revitalization have been essential in making this FotoFest happen. Gerard "Jordy" Tollett, director of Houston's Convention and Entertainment Facilities Department, has been invaluable in many ways. We also want to thank Pete Radowick from that department. Without the assistance of Jackie Alfred, executive administrator of the city's Theater District Association, we could not have done the street marking program downtown. Nancy Brainerd, president of the Downtown Houston Association, helped us promote FotoFest downtown. Jim Maxwell and Steve Filippo of the Downtown Historic District helped with many contacts in the Market Square area. Once again, we turned to Central Houston and the Downtown District for advice and assistance, particularly Guy Hagstette, Diann Lewter and Ashley Smith. Jessica Cusick, director of the Public Art Program for the Cultural Arts Council, provided insight and advice on many occasions.

With the other arts organizations, we worked closely with many people. In particular, we want to thank María Inéz Sicardi and Jim Sanders for the many ways in which they and their gallery have supported the philosophy and presentation of FotoFest. Rick Lowe and Deborah Grotfeldt provided one of our closest collaborations with Project Row Houses. Mike Golden, director of the Art Department at Houston Community College Central, made the Vietnam show possible. Among the shows in corporate spaces, the collaborations with Sally Sprout at Transco Tower and

Jennifer Childress at One Allen Center were very beneficial to the festival. Linda Haag Carter and the Art League of Houston provided the Month of Photography with a very special show. Kimberly Davenport of Rice University Gallery always brings innovative programs to Houston and the Gary Hill collaboration is no exception. Michelle Barnes at Community Artists Collective made it possible to bring a new African American artist to Houston for FotoFest. We worked with the Houston Center for Photography (HCP) in many ways, and Jean Caslin contributed not only one but two shows to FotoFest 98 through HCP's collaboration with the Goethe Institute. Emily Todd and DiverseWorks Artspace provided one of the festival's most important exhibitions as well as a special evening for out-of-town guests at the exhibition site. The participation of the Orange Show was a wonderful addition to the festival this year. We are also grateful for Sally Reynolds' long involvement with FotoFest and her show at Wells Fargo Plaza. The support of the Colquitt, Museum District and Upper Kirby galleries in exhibitions and their group opening nights is very important to FotoFest. The participation of galleries in the Heights, West University and Galleria give the festival its citywide dimension.

Aside from the curators, many individuals have helped with the exhibitions: Consul General of Peru Jorge Salas, Dr. Keith McElroy, and Fernando Castro with the Eugène (Eugenio) Courret exhibition from Peru; David Thomas of the Indochina Arts Project, Ralph Samuelson of the Asian Cultural Council and Abby Robinson with the Vietnam show; Richard Lanier of the Trust for Mutual Understanding and Dr. Miroslav Musil of the Embassy of Slovakia in Washington D.C. with the shows from Slovakia; Diane Auberger from Magnum Photos in Paris with the Harry Gruyaert show; Kathy Vargas of the Guadalupe Cultural Arts Center with the Spirits and Constructions show; Patricia Mendoza, Julieta Jimenez Cacho, and Gabriela Gonzales from the Centro de la Imagen with the show from Mexico; Eugenio Valdés Figueroa with the show from South Africa; and Jane Lombard and Leah Freid with the Danny Tisdale show.

Longtime staff member and exhibitions coordinator Diane Barber helped give us a good start last year before she went to a new career with Diverseworks. Her place was ably taken by Leigh Martinez, who had to compress years of experience into a few months. Martha Skow's success in coordinating both the International Meeting Place and the Fine Print Auction is reflected in the fact that the Meeting Place was sold out four months in advance. Even with a young son in tow, Marta Sánchez Philippe managed to help with countless tasks, from coordinating press in Latin America, to the Meeting Place, the Auction, and the Latin American book. Coming to work in the last months before the festival, Cristine Rosales did much to make the office and press work run smoothly. Tammy Johnson and Sue Tyler's work with office operations was essential.

Leslie Johnson did a marvelous job coordinating the 1998 catalogue, and Michelle Nichols' editing of the catalogue text was superb.

It was a real pleasure to work with Pennebaker Design on the design and production of the catalogue, brochures, and other festival exhibition publications. David Lerch did the design and Rochelle Freedman supervised production. Masterpiece Litho once again did a wonderful printing job for both the festival and auction catalogues as well as most of our other publications.

Susan Elmore not only worked on press, but also helped with openings, downtown public relations, and sponsorships. As always, it was a delight to work with her and her assistant Sammye Rusco.

The exhibition designers are a particularly good team of people who worked on contract. Working on his fifth Month of Photography, set designer Jim Kanan helped transform the building spaces into functioning galleries and did the design for the markers. Keith Hollingsworth did the matting and framing for the exhibitions.

The team of Karen Bering, Lisa Mathis, and El Matha Wilder created one of the most successful fundraising auctions FotoFest has ever presented. Beth Carls, Amy Cooper, Stephanie Owens, and Keith Nickerson from Align Solutions did a wonderful job with the production of the auction catalogue. Without Arturo Sánchez' hard work, the matting of the auction prints could not have happened. Peter Yenne helped with catalogue photography for the auction.

The International Meeting Place could not run without a small army of volunteers. John and Carola Herrin and Jake and Betty Mooney head this group. They have given the Meeting Place many hours of assistance as well as valuable organizational insight.

The ongoing successes of the *Literacy Through Photography* program and the organization of the new charter school, Kaleidoscope, were the result of the work of LTP director David Brown and LTP curriculum consultant Marie Scanlin.

A very special thanks to Wendy Ramires, Marcia Carter, and Ruth Teleki for serving as FotoFest's volunteer team for our school tour program. Their commitment to this complex project helped make it possible for several thousand Houston school children to tour, study, and explore FotoFest 98 exhibitions.

There are personal friends without whose support and advice FotoFest would not have survived as long and as well as it has. We want to particularly thank Louisa Stude Sarofim, Jane Blaffer Owen, Mary Porter, Miles Glaser, Susan Garwood, and Marcia Carter.

And we are very grateful for the extraordinary hospitality of Roy and Mary Cullen, Jim and Sherry Kempner.

FOTOFEST 98

EXHIBITION

MAP

e and Dung Ngo of the Rice School of
ted a fun and funky streetscape design
Market Square with the Theater District.
tween FotoFest and the Theater District
rol into art.

EXHIBITIONS ORGANIZED BY FOTOFEST

PERFORMANCE

EXHIBITS

ORGANIZED BY

FOTOFEST

ALTERED WORLDS

Contemporary Slovak Staged Photography

ARTISTS: ROBO KOCAN, PAVEL PECHA, RUDO PREKOP, VASIL STANKO, MIRO SVOLÍK, KAMIL VARGA, PETER ZUPNÍK

Photography is… visual science fiction… intuition… dream… frozen time and space…
Ikko Narahara, Contemporary Photographers, 1982

The staged images, the manipulation of reality, self-projection, the spontaneous game, the new mythology, are typical of post-modern photography at the end of the 80s where "photography accepts worlds as an endless hall of mirrors, as a place where all we know are images…"
Andy Grundberg, Art News 1989

A defining characteristic of Slovak and Czech post-modern photography is the "Slovak New Wave," known at home and abroad through staged projects from the late 1980s by photographers Miro Svolík, Rudo Prekop, Tono Stano, Jano Pavlik (died 1988), Kamil Varga, Peter Zupník, and Vasil Stanko. Besides their photographic work, these artists belonged to the same generation, born about 1960. "This generational vaulting means for me, firstly, people with whom I have understanding. Even when each of us was doing something completely different it actually was a 'wave' wherein it was not necessary to explain everything because we were all on the same wavelength," Peter Zupník explains.

This belated Czecho-Slovak photographic postmodernism was brought to life by innovative photographic processes—theatrical and scenic effects and arrange-ments, luminography, the use of paint, and the like—used by these artists in the then stagnating domestic photographic scene, paralyzed by everyday political repression and the censorship of the failing "normal-ization" of 1970s socialism. After finishing their studies at FAMU (School of Film and Television) in Prague and following the later division of Czecho-Slovakia in 1993, most of these photographers remained in Prague. Despite different human and artistic destinies, they were classified and given a niche in art history as the "New Wavers."

Two other artists linked to these New Wavers are Pavel Pecha and Robo Kocan. Pecha belongs to the same generation and has many parallels in his creative work. Kocan represents the youngest generation of Slovak photographers. Although the main body of his work is mixed-media photography, the constructed landscapes in this exhibition are part of the spirit of the New Wave.

Large-scale theatrical settings dominate the works of both Pecha and Stanko. They create complex photo-theatrical scenarios, using precisely organized steps to execute each image. Pecha's series, *My Intuitive Theater* (1990-) is a narrative surrealistic affirmation of a world which reflects the artist's dreams and parodies reality. "I live in two worlds," Pecha says. "One is real and the other is like an alternative produced from a negative of the real world's vices. This one has greater value for me. It is a mirror or a picture of myself. It is a better and more perfect world than the real one. It is filled with fantasy, absurd situations, and games. Occasionally it is determined by the real world. Then violence and evil also appear. It serves me as a mirror of the real world".

Stanko's photographic "performances" are organized rituals in abandoned places inspired by dance, theater, and music. The human figures are in static or symbolic poses, always in two compositional planes. His photographic cycles (*The Heads*, 1991; *Half In, Half Out*, 1993; *Legs and Tales*, 1995; *Theater in the Mirrors*, 1996; *Pictures*, 1997) are sequences of images staged and directed by the photographer. "I am often unable to express in one photograph the whole idea which flows into the picture. Therefore I create a series of approximately ten images," Stanko explains. "The series are the result of previous ideas and concepts, which grow in me. I put together quite complicated images. The nude seems to me the purest and, at the same time, the most difficult. A person never attracts me as an object, neither in his/her physiognomy nor in terms of sex. The interest for me lies only in his/her activity—in the moment . . ."

Work with light, or luminography, is the major element in Kocan's fictional landscapes, the series *Drawings with Light and Returning* (1993-). "At the beginning of the 1990s, I produced unreal situations in selected nocturnal surroundings of the city where I was communicating only with myself," Kocan says. "From this black-and-white spectrum, I gradually moved to utilizing color. I began to look out for new inspiring surroundings. From the city I moved to the mountains and the wild countryside. With long exposures and with colored lighting, I draw dreamlike fictional landscapes in which imaginary fauna and flora come to life."

Luminography has also become fundamental to the work of Varga. His own body as well as abstract symbols are used to create an artistic dialogue with the universe. "I move gradually from cycle to cycle," Varga says. "The beginning cycle was *Autumn Psychotherapy and Other Experiences* (1989-90), then *ParaPortraits* (1990) and *New Topography* (1990-91). The first is about myself, then later the relationship of a person to the universe, and then about the nature of the universe itself. The person is a point of departure, representing his/her place, as a component of the universe." In the later series *Spirals* (1991-94), shown in this exhibition, a mystical light is given the dominant role. In content, the Spirals are the notes of certain psyche associations. Varga is considering himself as a mystic attempting to disclose the depths of the human soul and gain understanding of the secret laws of the universe. He does not perceive these images as "artistic works," but "more as a recognition of our subconscious. If I have to give a title to my way of working, I would call it 'spiritual expressionism,'" he says.

Fabricated photographs are typical for the work of Svolík. The cycle *Animals and People* (1992-96) contains compositions of tiny human figures mixed with landscapes and fragments of animal and human bodies. As in previous series by Svolík, this cycle is characterized by playfulness, humor, and poetry. "My photographs," Svolík says, "are basically black-and-white assemblages of landscapes and details of human and animal figures with arms, legs, fins, snake bodies, and so on. It is somewhat of a game, combining things together as the artistic expression of the conviction that everything is connected with everything. . . . I think I materialize feelings and thoughts suspended in the air. My photographs arise somehow from a state of self- submergence, half hypnosis . . ."

Prekop's series *Still Lives* (1990-97) are assemblages of miniature altars and slightly panoptic sculptures. This series, as well as *Homages and Monuments* is involved with philosophy and relationships to nature, its iconography, and the interpretations of values. "In *Still Lives*," Prekop explains, "the elements which compose these constructions are things which I find mostly in rubbish dumps. First I am interested in transparent things, objects which I put together and photograph under the heading of a leitmotif." Still Lives are microworlds which emerge in complex and ritualistic ways for only a moment, the moment of exposure, and then vanish forever.

Zupník is considered the most poetic photographer of the Slovak New Wave. He differs from his contemporaries of his generation in that he does not stage his photographs. Instead, he seeks snapshots with which he can conjure spontaneous tales and magical, playful fantasies about all manner of things. On most of his photographs, he draws with soft pastel strokes and creates a unique image. "I reflect on things that are no more," he says. "I think of people who are gone forever and yet are within reach. I carry their pictures inside me. I cannot make their pictures, so I go on searching in the Lands of Feelings . . I like stories."

Lucia Benická, Curator
House of Photography
Poprad, Slovakia

This exhibition was produced with the help of the House of Photography in Poprad, the Trust for Mutual Understanding, the Slovak Ministry of Foreign Relations, Embassy of Slovakia in Washington D.C., and the Foundation for a Civil Society. Presentation of the exhibit has been made possible by Harvey Seigle, Winter Street Art Center.

Sněžka - 1602 metrov nad morom
[Sněžka - 1602 Metres above Sea Level], 1994/1995
Miro Svolík
Silver Gelatin Print

My dvaja a cas [Two of us and the time], 1994/1995
Miro Svolík
Silver Gelatin Print

∑ *(dza)*, 1992
Kamil Varga
Cibachrome Print

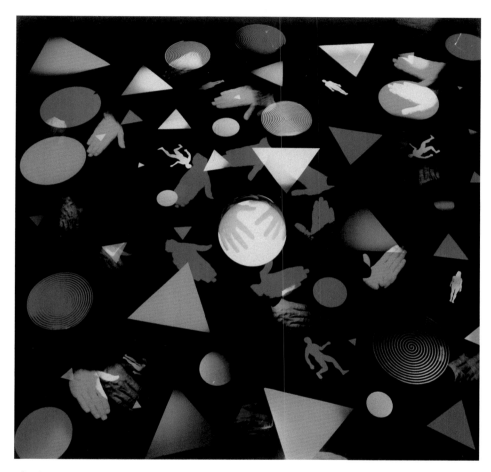

△⊥ (na), 1992
Kamil Varga
Cibachrome Print

from the series *My Intuitive Theater*, 1990-1997
Pavel Pecha
Toned Silver Gelatin Print

from the series *My Intuitive Theater*, 1990-1997
Pavel Pecha
Toned Silver Gelatin Print

Hitchockove vtáky [Hitchcock's Birds], 1995
Robo Kočan
Cibachrome Print

Odkliaty hrad [Disenchanted Castle], 1995
Robo Kočan
Cibachrome Print

Sen o kolobezkách [The Dream about Scooters], 1992
Peter Zupník
Hand-painted Silver Gelatin Print

Icarus [Self-portrait], 1992
Peter Zupník
Hand-painted Silver Gelatin Print

Pomník Noemoved Arche [Monument to Noah's Ark], 1993
Rudo Prekop
Silver Gelatin Print

Pocta rastlinám [Hommage to Flowers], 1991-1997
Rudo Prekop
Silver Gelatin Print

from the *Windows* series, 1991-1997
Vasil Stanko
Silver Gelatin Print

from the *Head* series, 1991-1997
Vasil Stanko
Hand Colored Silver Gelatin Print

FOTOFEST EXHIBIT

LOOKING AT THE 90's

Four Views of Current Mexican Photography

Presented by AT&T

JOSÉ ANTONIO RODRÍGUEZ

ARTISTS: LAURA BARRÓN ECHAURI, XIMENA BERECOCHEA
FERNÁNDEZ, ADRIANA CALATAYUD MORÁN, MARIANNA
DELLEKAMP, GERARDO MONTIEL KLINT

Visions of the Twenty-first Century

Much has happened in Mexican photography during the 1990s. We have already gone a long way, a very long way, from the nationalistic references that were Mexican photography's trademark abroad for so many years. Current Mexican photography is establishing new pathways. These pathways are, in turn, the result of a neo-avant garde movement that emerged at the end of the seventies and came to maturity in the eighties.

That situation favored the development of a dynamic movement of diverse visual experimentation in the 1990s, principally represented by young photographers born in the second half of the sixties. In the nineties, we see an unusual boom in photography, sometimes moving in the direction of excessive self-representation, or mise-en-scène, constructed photography, or the mixing of photography with other media such as digital images, video, and installation that had become natural points of conjunction by the end of the century. There was also a certain decline in documentary photography, a return to old printing techniques—*papel salado* (salt paper process), platinum, cyanotype, gum bichromate—and the revival of older and seldom used photographic genres such as the landscape.

The photographers presented in this part of the exhibition represent only a small selection, made from a very particular point of view, of what has been happening in Mexican photography in recent years. These are photographers who are exploring different forms of sensory expression in the direction of new world views. All of them display a certain note of desolation and sadness. Laura Barrón and Ximena Berecochea return to the landscape—a genre almost abandoned in the eighties except for a few sporadic cases—and they reappropriate it. Barrón uses a stylistic aesthetic marked by a desolate grandiloquence. Berecochea creates intimate microstructures that look to memory more than to immediate experience. Gerardo Montiel Klint develops fantasy-like displays of marine zoology that he converts into totems which seem like precursors to the altars of a new century. Adriana Calatayud displays the interior structures of the body and their fragility as part of the body's inevitable decline towards death. In her return to the origins of life, Marianna Dellekamp retreats into an idyllic, protective, and uninhibited microuniverse, seeking to envelope the spectator in a world that has already been lost.

These are very personal and fictional visions of the end of this century. However, if they are looked at carefully, it may be seen that they do not belong to the twentieth century, but rather to the century that follows. In this work, we see the evidence of what has been left: desolation, the last remnants of altars, the vulnerability of the body, the last places of refuge. It is a photographic fiction without hope, a vision that appears to offer us no alternative exit.

José Antonio Rodríguez
Independent curator, photo historian and critic

 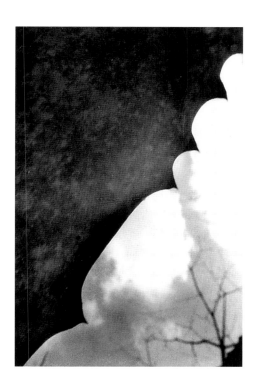

Sin título, de la serie *En aire*,
[*Untitled*, from the series *In the Air*] 1996
Ximena Berecochea
Diptych
Silver Gelatin Print

de la serie, *Paradeísos II*,
[from the series, *Paradises II*] 1997
Laura Barrón
Toned Silver Gelatin Print

de la serie, *Paradeísos III,*
[from the series, *Paradises III*] 1997
Laura Barrón
Toned Silver Gelatin Print

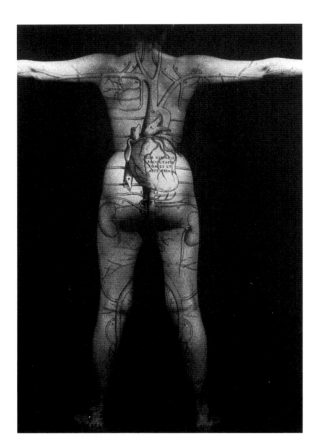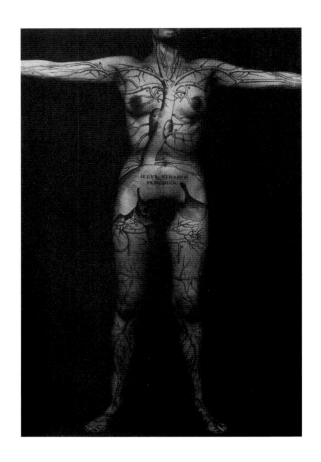

de la serie, *Monografías,*
[from the series, *Monographs*], 1995
Adriana Calatayud Morán
Diptych
Silver Gelatin Print

del proyecto, *In situ*,
[from the project, *On Site*], 1995
Marianna Dellekamp
Digital Print

del proyecto, *In situ*,
[from the project, *On Site*], 1996
Marianna Dellekamp
Digital Print

Totem y Tabú II, de la serie *El Sueño*,
[*Totem and Taboo II*, from the series *The Dream*], 1995
Gerardo Montiel Klint
Toned Silver Gelatin Print

Totem y Tabú III, de la serie *El Sueño*,
[*Totem and Taboo III*, from the series *The Dream*], 1995
Gerardo Montiel Klint
Toned Silver Gelatin Print

ANA CASAS

ARTISTS: KATYA BRAILOWSKY PLATA, MAYA GODED COLICHIO, JAVIER RAMÍREZ LIMÓN, MARUCH SANTÍZ GÓMEZ, DANIEL WEINSTOCK ARENOVITZ

You could not look Medusa in the face because you would turn to stone. The hero who killed her used a mirror to divert her petrified stare towards herself. The little disposable camera has been my protection, and photography the reflection that has defended me from Medusa's stare.
Katya Brailowsky

Photography's relationship with external reality differentiates it from other media. The camera opens a path between the eye and the world while simultaneously revealing a new and surprising reality. The fragment of time captured in a photo reveals the mystery of the interaction between the photographer and outside reality, exposing the fascinating threshold between the interior and the exterior, between reality and representation.

The five artists selected here share a vital commitment to photography and imagery that is essentially photographic. Their work allows contemplation of the internal workings of a photograph without necessary recourse to other media. Through the act of photography, these artists are engaged in an exploration of reality. In different ways, the work of each one of these artists exists only at this point of engagement, giving rise to a new and singular reality and immersing us in the ambiguity of existence.

Javier Ramírez Limón deliberately disturbs the traditional boundaries of portraiture in subtle and transgressive ways. In a seemingly simple photographic game, he reconstructs his family and relatives by photographing his friends and strangers in poses that he remembers from his parents and siblings. The facial expressions of his subjects are very intense, as if the

interior and the exterior are momentarily merged. But the person photographed is also another person, thereby exposing another mystery and the elusive threshold between one self and the other. Ramírez game goes even further because he creates a story: "In an old downtown hotel, I decided that my mother would be my lover and my father a stranger." He leads us suddenly to another space where a narrative breaks the boundaries of representation and engages in an even more dangerous game.

In Daniel Weinstock Arenovitz' images, reality rearranges itself in oddly theatrical scenes. His photographs do not portray theatrical works: they are the play itself, theatrical acts that do not exist outside the characters themselves. Through an intense interrelationship with external reality, Weinstock's images are a perfect extension of his line of vision and lead us into a world where everything fits mysteriously together. The photographs are born from encounters with people who are the protagonists of stories in Weinstock's world. They exist in an enigmatic space between his own fantasy and the dramatic reality of his characters' own lives.

Katya Brailowsky Plata immerses us in a personal vision of the world wherein she captures moments that seem to come from a child's innocent, sometimes cruel way of looking at the world. There is a certain purity in this vision that appears straightforward in the beginning but little by little takes us inside a profound reflection on the nature of reality and photography. As in her texts, the conceptual aspect of her photography is indissolubly connected to the existential experiences that give birth to her images.

Maya Goded Colichio has been working for several years with prostitutes in Mexico City. Following their own fantasies and obsessions, she gets close to these women and photographs them in their hotel rooms.

Although she comes from documentary photography, she breaks important boundaries in this genre. The harshness of her subject may provoke the spectator, but the true transgression of Goded's work is how she lets us see inside her own way of looking at these women. The women being portrayed are in front of the photographer looking at her, sometimes trying to seduce her, other times provoking her while assuming different poses. In the staring eyes of these women, we confront the artist's stare and our own as well. Goded's photographs take us into the photographic act in its purest sense because they reveal the author's internal search in her confrontation with the prostitutes. Goded neither overwhelms the presence of the women nor tries to reach conclusions; rather, she reflects the ambiguity and intensity of the experience as well as the sensual pleasure of the experience and the pleasure of transgression.

In her photographs, Maruch Santíz Gómez presents us with a vision that differs from what we are used to seeing in photography, and she does it very differently from the other artists in this selection. Santíz is an Indian from Chiapas. She uses photography to represent her village traditions with the intention of preserving and transmitting them for illiterate people. Her images clearly represent a different way of seeing objects. Together with her texts, we are given the impression that another world is opening up to our perception. It is her vision, and photography is the way we can see that vision. The images surprise us: we do not know if the surprise comes from the artist's way of seeing or from the presence of a different culture that escapes our ability to interpret it.

The photographs of these artists come from a deep need to affirm life. Photography gives them access to existentially risky, sometimes hidden, worlds and experiences. But their images are not documents of an alien reality; they come from a direct confrontation between the "I" and "the other." This photography is nourished by the need to penetrate and touch external reality, the desire to find one's own identity through this confrontation, and finally the wish to cross that elusive threshold into another reality.

Ana Casas
Educational coordinator and photographer
Centro de la Imagen, Mexico City

This exhibition is presented by AT&T, with assistance from the Centro de la Imagen and its director, Patricia Mendoza, in Mexico City. The presentation of the exhibit has been made possible by Fletcher Thorne-Thomson, Jr., Vine Street Studios.

de la serie, *Bajo un mismo cielo*,
[from the series, *Under the Same Sky*], 1994-1996
Daniel Weinstock
Silver Gelatin Print

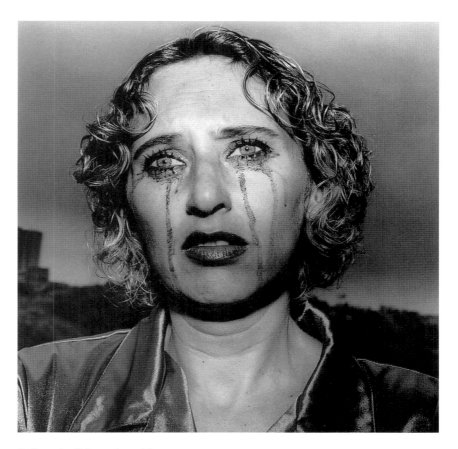

de la serie, *Bajo un mismo cielo*,
[from the series, *Under the Same Sky*], 1994-1996
Daniel Weinstock
Silver Gelatin Print

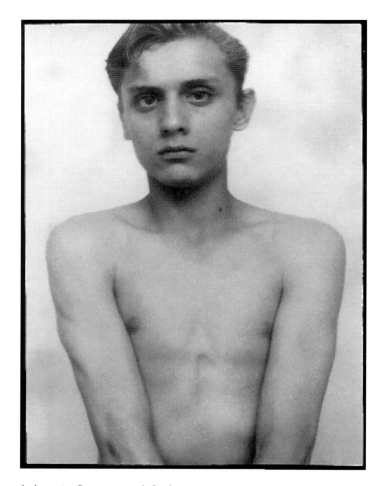

de la serie, *Reconstrucción de familia,*
[from the series, *Family Reconstruction*], 1996
Javier Ramírez Limón
Platinum Print

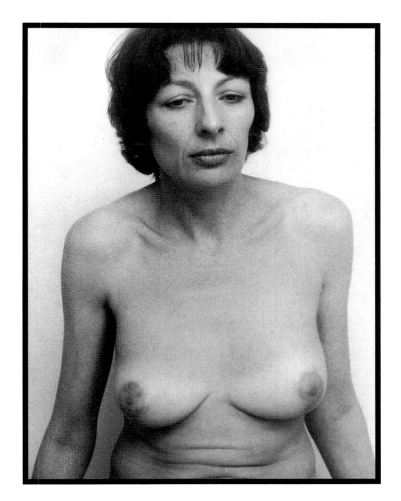

de la serie, *Reconstrucción de familia,*
[from the series, *Family Reconstruction*], 1996
Javier Ramírez Limón
Platinum Print

En casa de la tía de Pavka,
[In the House of the Aunt of Pavka], 1997
Katya Brailowsky
Cibachrome Print

La santa muerte,
[Sainted Death], 1997
Katya Brailowsky
Cibachrome Print

TZ'UJUB
No sentarse donde gotea el techo, de la serie *Creencias de Chamula*,
[*Don't sit where drops fall from the roof* from the series, *Chamula Beliefs*], 1995-1996
Maruch Santíz Gómez
Silver Gelatin Print

Tz'ujub - *No sentarse donde cae gotera del techo*

Mu xtun xijchotiotik ta yalob tz'ujub, yu'un chijpas ta jtub
ik', xchi'uk mi o'lol xa k'ak'ale mu xtun xijchotiotik
yu'un mu xa xij'alaj mu xa xijnich'naj o.

*Es malo sentarse donde cae gotera del techo, porque te
puede dar a uno enfermedad de ataque. Además cuando a
las 12 del día en punto se sienta uno en el lugar ya
mencionado se puede quedar estéril.*

PISBIL BATZ'I NO
El estambre de lana, de la serie *Creencias de Chamula,*
[*Wool Yarn* from the series, *Chamula Beliefs*], 1994-1996
Maruch Santíz Gómez
RC Print

Pisbil batz'i no - *El estambre de pelota*

Mu xtun xich' jipolanel ta ixtolanel li pisbil batz'i noe, mi
yich' ixtolanele mu xlok'oj o jlik k'u'il, ak'o mi volabil ti
jayvol ono'ox chich'e, yu'un la chbat ta ik' li sch'ulel
tzotze.

Es malo jugar como pelota con el estambre de lana; si se
juega así, no va salir completa una prenda de cualquier
tamaño, aunque se haya contado cuántos pares lleva cada
prenda, porque se dice que al espíritu de la lana se lo va
llevar el viento.

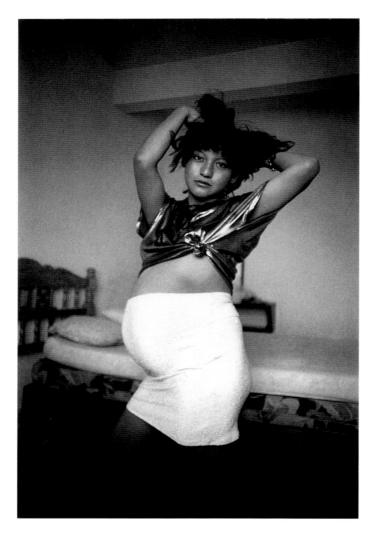

de la serie, *En un cuarto de hotel,*
[from the series, *In a Hotel Room],* 1995-1997
Maya Goded
Silver Gelatin Print

de la serie, *En un cuarto de hotel,*
[from the series, *In a Hotel Room],* 1995-1997
Maya Goded
Silver Gelatin Print

OSVALDO SÁNCHEZ

ARTISTS: PÍA ELIZONDO, EDGAR LADRÓN DE GUEVARA, SEBASTIÁN RODRÍGUEZ ROMO

With the outstanding exception of Muralism and starting precisely with that movement, Mexican photography has been the preferred source of that range of symbols which has catalogued and constructed "lo mexicano" ("Mexicanness") as the utopian ideal of national identity, configuring it with a self-imposed exoticism and legitimizing its cliches as the guarantees of its authenticity, the official "Bildung" of Mexico, mestizo and modern. The weight of this construct has burdened Mexican photography for years and enveloped it within a well-known rhetoric. This extends to the subjects of the recent avant-garde: the body and its elements, postmodern references to the prehispanic past, and the fragile perseverance of the hidden underside of Mexico ("México profundo") awaiting decolonialization. These images have effectively replaced the old motifs without disturbing the inertia of a systemic national vision, desirous of documenting its own exoticism.

My interest in selecting these three artists who work with photography today in Mexico focuses on the overabundance of that national vision and my desire to bring into evidence new areas of discourse: discourse that is not trying to create small Mexican icons out of images—whether it be the body, landscape, or an anthropological narrative—destined to service a system of representation that can be easily integrated and manipulated within the dominant circles of cultural interpretation.

Pía Elizondo, Edgar Ladrón de Guevara, and Sebastián Rodríguez Romo are grouped together to show the existence of another way of looking in Mexican photography, one that is not straightforward, one that looks for minimalist spaces and what is tangential and fluid. It focuses on what is not in focus—where the invisible, the absent, and the unclassifiable are the categories of reference. This way of looking undoubtedly comes from experience with video and the imminence of a virtual age. It is a liquescent gaze, whose strategy feigns malleability. These are specific and particular visions, not emblematic ones. They bypass and countermand advertising's demand to "look at me."

In the context of the zoo, Elizondo has tracked the comfortable artifice of the postmodern habitat, the "cyberhome" or commercial stage set, where domesticity adorns itself with exoticism and solitude is disguised as a mark of distinction. Ladrón de Guevara shows us a way of looking that is similar to what Rosanna Stone calls the "vampire's look." His visual deconstructions seem to lead us into the construct of what is tangible. There is a merging of his vision and what is barely in flux into a type of "bloodlust." Rodríguez constructs minimalist landscapes out of urban waste and discarded objects that are not "worth the trouble."

Osvaldo Sánchez
Independent curator and writer

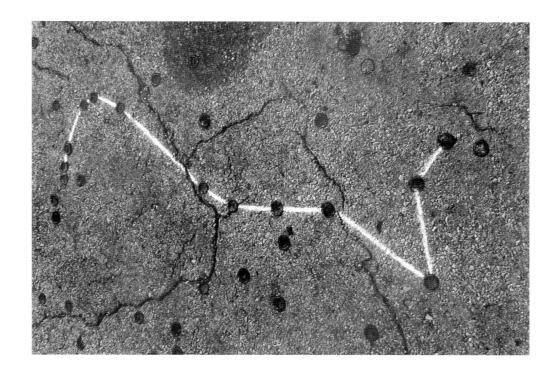

Constelaciones [Constellations], 1997
Sebastián Rodríguez
Silver Gelatin Prints

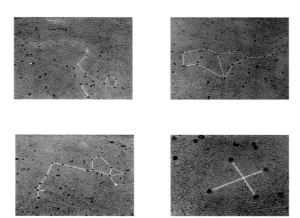

de la serie, *El beso esencial,*
[from the series, *The Essential Kiss*], 1995-96
Edgar Ladrón de Guevara
Toned Silver Gelatin Print

de la serie, *El beso esencial,*
[from the series, *The Essential Kiss*], 1995-96
Edgar Ladrón de Guevara
Toned Silver Gelatin Print

Sin título de la serie, *Zoológico*, 1997
[*Untitled* from the series, *Zoological*]
Pía Elizondo
Silver Gelatin Print

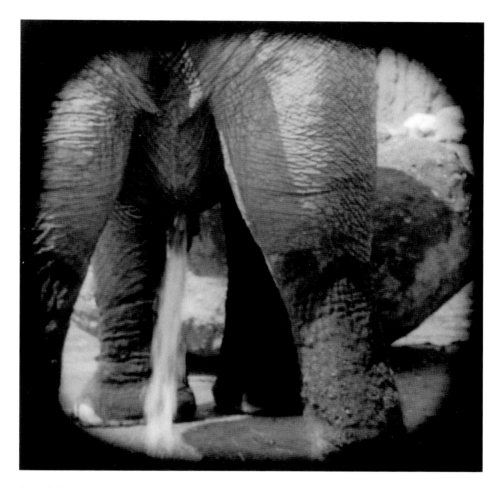

Sin título de la serie, *Zoológico*, 1997
[*Untitled* from the series, *Zoological*]
Pía Elizondo
Silver Gelatin Print

MIGUEL FEMATT

ARTISTS: MARCO ANTONIO CRUZ, CARLOS JURADO, DANIEL MENDOZA, HILDEGART MORENO OLOARTE, PEDRO SLIM

The Eclectic Nineties

It is true that in the nineties photography has found new directions with techniques such as the use of laser printing, or the latest artistic idiom such as installations. It is also true that these new paths continue to coexist with old techniques and precepts.

In my curatorial work for this exhibition, I decided to bring together five different ways of approaching photography to show that at the end of this century, when globalization is more than demagogic discourse, time and space seem to come together in unprecedented ways.

Photography has been a technique used not only by artists in creating images, but also by photographers for utilitarian purposes—documentation, publicity, science, journalism, an so on. In the same way that old nineteenth-century artisanal techniques have made a comeback, important documentary work in the 1990s continues to record the eternal pagan rituals of the indigenous peoples of Mexico with the same persistence that characterizes the survival of these cultures. As a documentary photographer, Daniel Mendoza expresses his vision of the world as a series of evanescent moments imbued with a "Mexican" magic, while he uses the most classical forms of photographic expression.

Marco Antonio Cruz, who started as a photojournalist, now devotes his time to creating documentary essays on subjects that fascinate him. His book *Cafetaleros* is a formal denunciation of the current situation of the Indians in Chiapas. The selection presented in this exhibition is another essay about blind people in Mexico City, a theme that has been important to all photographers.

Carlos Jurado, a painter, has a long-standing interest in the craft of photography. In this context, he created an academic project in 1975 at the University of Veracruz called Tecnología Alternativa (Alternative Technology), wherein he simultaneously researched, experimented, and took pictures with the camera oscura (pinhole camera), exploiting all its potential. His current work is the result of many years of work and a clear vision as to the direction of his explorations.

From the basis of his interest in the male nude, Pedro Slim works with the most straightforward form of photographic portraiture to photograph young gang members in his studio using even lighting and a black background. Although his influences are obvious, he brings to our eyes and our minds a different way of looking at people whom we believed to be only delinquents.

Hildegart Moreno Oloarte is the youngest of the artists I have chosen, and she is the one who uses the most contemporary idiom. Her installation *Ensayo para la realidad* (*Essay on Reality*) synthesizes the feeling of hopelessness about the future that many young people of her generation share. She states that: "I could not find a better way to represent them."

As a professor of photography at the university level, I have to pay attention to all kinds of different interests among my students. On a daily basis, I also have to review the history of photography as a technical and artistic language. This is why I agree with Susan Sontag when she said that in literature one can be eclectic up to a certain point, but that it is impossible for someone to like everything equally. In photography, however, there is no limit to being eclectic (or to eclecticism).

Miguel Fematt
Director of the photography program at the University of Veracruz and the Festival of Photography in Xalapa.

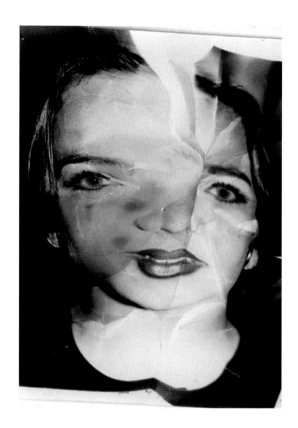

Ensayo para la realidad
[Essay on Reality], 1997
Hildegart Moreno Oloarte
Silver Gelatin Prints from Mixed Media
Installation

Ahorcadito con vaso
[Hanged Skeleton with Glass], 1996 copied 1997
Carlos Jurado
Silver Gelatin Print

Ahorcadito en la bañera
[Hanged Skeleton in the Bathtub], 1996 copied 1997
Carlos Jurado
Silver Gelatin Print

de la serie, *Ciegos*
[from the series, *Blind People*], 1987-1997
Marco Antonio Cruz
Silver Gelatin Print

de la serie, *Ciegos*
[from the series, *Blind People*], 1987-1997
Marco Antonio Cruz
Silver Gelatin Print

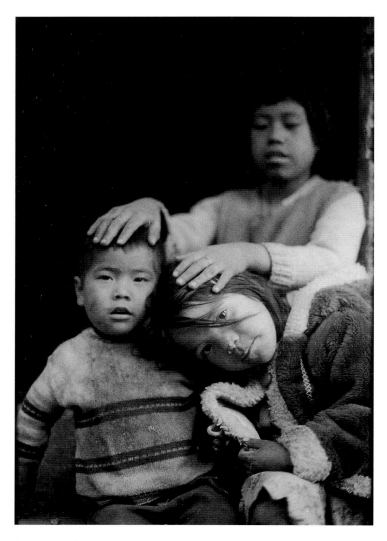

de la serie, *San Miguel Aguasuelos, un pueblo alfarero*
[from the series, *San Miguel Aguasuelos, a Village of Ceramicists*], 1986-1989
Daniel Mendoza
Silver Gelatin Print

de la serie, *San Miguel Aguasuelos, un pueblo alfarero*
[from the series, *San Miguel Aguasuelos, a Village of Ceramicists*], 1986-1989
Daniel Mendoza
Silver Gelatin Print

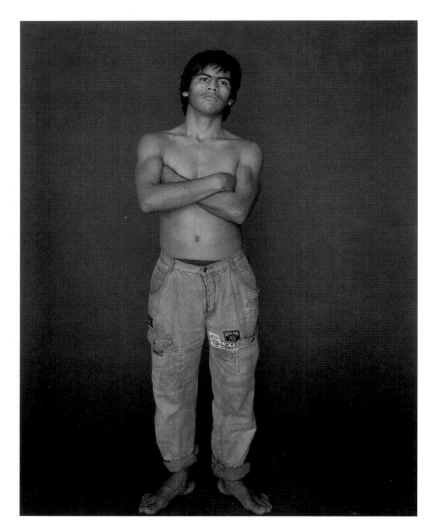

de la serie, *De la calle al estudio*
[from the series, *From the Street to the Studio*], 1993-1997
Pedro Slim
Silver Gelatin Print

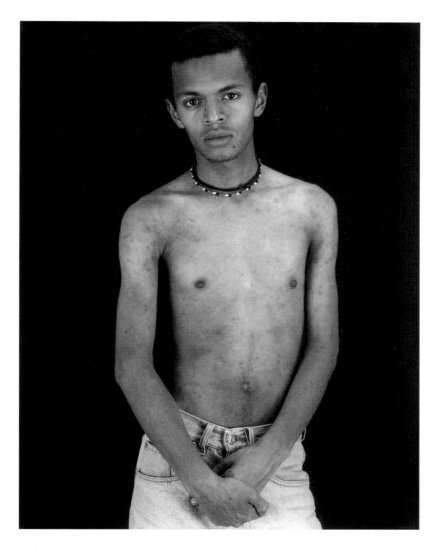

de la serie, *De la calle al estudio,*
[from the series, *From the Street to the Studio*], 1993-1997
Pedro Slim
Silver Gelatin Print

DISCOVERIES OF THE MEETING PLACE

ARTISTS: JAN CAMP, VALDIR CRUZ, DEBORAH HAMMOND, KATE MELLOR, ANNE ARDEN MCDONALD, PHILIPPE PACHE, ORVILLE ROBERTSON, ADRIENE VENINGER, FREDERIC WEBER, FRANK YAMRUS

Created by photographers for photographers, FotoFest's International Meeting Place is intended as a place for discovery. It is a place where the usual barriers between artists and art institutions are diminished—where photographic artists meet and show work on a one-to-one basis to curators and directors from important art spaces around the world. At FotoFest, portfolio reviews at the Meeting Place are open to anyone who wants to register. There is no pre-selection process, no prior review. Over the past ten years, registrants at the Meeting Place have had the opportunity to interact with representatives of almost every major photography institution and publication in the United States, Europe, Canada, Latin America, Japan, and parts of the Middle East. Given the range of reviewers from museums, galleries, photo agencies, artist spaces, newspapers, and magazines, the Meeting Place provides an unparalleled opportunity for photographers wanting to show their work to important people in the photographic art field.

To honor this process of discovery, FotoFest is sponsoring the second Discoveries of the Meeting Place exhibition. This exhibition is dedicated solely to work by artists who participated in FotoFest's 1996 International Meeting Place portfolio reviews. The artists included in the exhibition were selected by individual curators who worked at the 1996 Meeting Place. We asked them to send FotoFest the names of photographers whom they discovered at the Meeting Place and whose work they found particularly interesting.

FotoFest and the Meeting Place are fortunate to have the services of many of the most experienced curators and critics in the world of photography. The portfolio reviewers work long hours during the eight days of the Meeting Place. Without their expertise and commitment to photography, the Meeting Place could not function.

The Discoveries of the Meeting Place is an ongoing part of the FotoFest exhibitions program at FotoFest's biennial International Month of Photography. The Meeting Place is one of the most important programs FotoFest offers to photographic artists. The opportunity to exhibit is another dimension of the exposure available to Meeting Place participants.

Fred Baldwin and Wendy Watriss
FotoFest

Presentation of this exhibition is made possible by Kathy Nelson, Erie City Ironworks.

The artists and curators:

Jan Camp (United States) recommended by
Andy Grundberg, independent critic and curator,
San Francisco, California

Valdir Cruz (United States/Brazil) recommended by
María Teresa García Pedroche, assistant curator at the
Meadows Museum, Dallas, Texas

Deborah Hammond (United States) recommended by
José Ignacio Roca, curator at Luis Angel Arango
Library, Banco de la Republica, Bogota, Colombia

Kate Mellor (United Kingdom) recommended by
Tina Schelhorn, director of Internationale Szene,
Cologne, Germany

Anne Arden McDonald (United States)
recommended by Marcel Blouin, director of Mois de
la Photo, Montreal

Philippe Pache (Switzerland) recommended by
Patricia Mendoza, director of the Centro de la
Imagen, Mexico City

Orville Robertson (United States) recommended by
Roland Charles, director of Black Gallery,
Los Angeles, California

Adriene Veninger (Canada) recommended by
John Cleary, director of John Cleary Gallery,
Houston, Texas

Frederic Weber (United States) recommended by
Adam Weinberg, curator of the permanent collection,
Whitney Museum, New York, New York

Frank Yamrus (United States) recommended by Sunil
Gupta, curator of the Organization for Visual Arts,
London

Untitled Self Portrait #55, 1994
Anne Arden McDonald
Silver Gelatin Print

Portrait # 22-10-94, 1994
Deborah Hammond
Silver Gelatin Print

TR 300395. Shakespeare Cliff, Dover, 1997
No. 1 from *Island: The Sea Front Series*
Kate Mellor
Type C Print

R.J. Bronze, 1994
Frank Yamrus
Silver Gelatin Print

Rachel, 1996
Philippe Pache
Toned Silver Gelatin Print

Leaf no.14 , from the *Folia* series, 1996
Adriene Veninger
Silver Gelatin Print

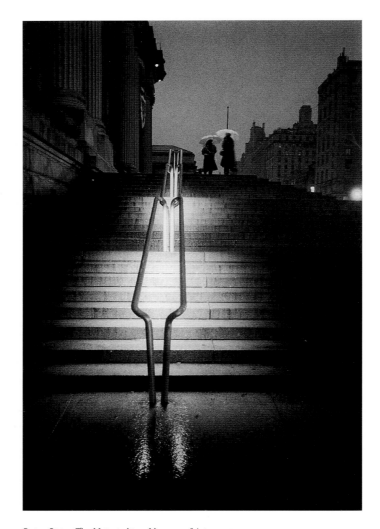

Rainy Steps, The Metropolitan Museum of Art, 1997
Orville Robertson
Silver Gelatin Print

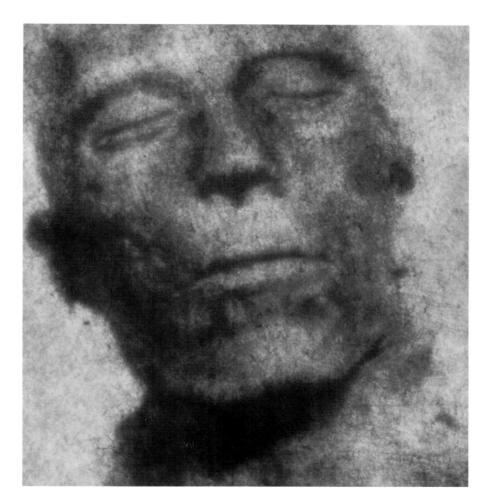

Untitled #80, 1995
Frederic Weber
Cibachrome Print

Spring, 1996
Jan Camp
Oil, Silver Print on Aluminum

"Jose Adalberto da Silva"
Leader Makuxi wearing a Karajá Necklace, 1995
Valdir Cruz
Selenium Toned Silver Gelatin Print

PENTTI SAMMALLAHTI

One of Finland's best-known photographers, Pentti Sammallahti describes himself as a "wanderer" who likes the nature of the great north, the silence, the cold, the sea, the people of far-off places, animals, and roadways. For three decades, he has traveled along the coasts of the Atlantic and the Arctic Oceans, throughout the Finnish Archipelago, and the remote villages of northern and eastern Europe.

In addition to Sammallahti's original prints from Russia, Finland, and Eastern Europe, this exhibition includes his handmade books, which demonstrate higly refined and complex printing and typographic techniques developed by the artist. Sammallahti is known in Scandinavia not only as a fine art photographer, but also as the originator and designer of his own books and the inventor of special photographic printing techniques and book graphics.

Wendy Watriss, FotoFest
Text excerpted from exhibition introduction at the Mois de la Photo, 1996.

This exhibition was produced in collaboration with the artist in conjunction with his exhibition at the Mois de la Photo in Paris in 1996. Presentation of the exhibition has received support from the Finnish government.

Solovki, White Sea, Russia, 1992
from the portfolio *The Russian Way*, 1996
Pentti Sammallahti
Silver Gelatin Print

Vuokkini, Carelia, Russia, 1991
from the portfolio *The Russian Way*, 1996
Pentti Sammallahti
Silver Gelatin Print

Solovki, White Sea, Russia, 1992
from the portfolio *The Russian Way,* 1996
Pentti Sammallahti
Silver Gelatin Print

FIVE SOUTH AFRICAN ARTISTS

ARTISTS: WILLIAM KENTRIDGE, PAT MAUTLOA, ZWELETHU MTHETHWA, PENNY SIOPSIS, SUE WILLIAMSON

Drawing upon a full range of visual media, five contemporary South African artists explore issues of history, identity, power, aesthetics, and community — personal and collective. All of these artists incorporate elements of still photography and cinematic imagery in these works, but they move beyond traditional definitions and norms of usage to develop new formats of expression.

Sue Williamson has created a large body of video, installation, and mixed-media work dealing with issues of slavery and bondage. For FotoFest 1998, she presents a recent work, *Truth Games* which she describes as a series of "game boards" that "attempts to replicate the experience of South Africans coming to grips with the horror stories surfacing in the Truth and Reconciliation Commission hearings." Each row of boards represents a particular case, incorporating Williamson's own photographs, media images, and strips of text on a grid. As viewers move or slide different sections of the "game boards," different aspects of these cases are revealed. "It will never be possible to see the whole board at once, since on each row of strips there will be a sliding panel with a small knob which viewers can slide across and cover one third of the row. 'Truth' will be in the eye of the beholder," Williamson says.

Pat Mautloa's work has roots in the history of black "township art" which traditionally depicted the more sentimental aspects of everyday township life for viewing in a fine arts context by primarily white South African audiences. Mautloa, however, eschews this tradition to give visibility to the harsher realities of township life. His installation re-creates the living and work spaces of squatter camps reflecting the economic hardships and oppression of migrant workers. "I use the wall as a metaphor. The walls can reflect--life inside and outside as a skin which covers the inside or the souls . . . I use color to reflect the hope that has vanished in people," Mautloa says.

In *Vanity at Frankie's*, Zwelethu Mthethwa's installation does focus on a more benign part of black South African township life, the barbershop. "On growing up as a black African male," Mthethwa says, "I had two options regarding cutting hair. It was cut either at home or by a local barber, which was regarded as a luxury. At home it would be cut using either a pair of scissors . . . or a razor blade. The local barber offered few styles at different hair lengths as well . . . For our black female counterparts, it was a different world. They had endless options . . . . [But] when the international hair products such as Revlon and Soft and Free were imported to South Africa in the late 1970s, hair vanity was never the same . . . . New attitudes toward hair and gender developed. Male vanity in hair became a hot debate . . . [Barbershops] also borrowed a lot of new hairstyles from the U.S. and West Africa. Men had the option of going to either the hair salons or the barbershops. Today the barbershop I go to is in Langa, a small township about twenty kilometers outside Cape Town . . . . My barber Frankie comes from Lagos, Nigeria. What is fascinating with him is the various unconventional instruments he employs in cutting hair. This led me to do a photographic project on his barbershop."

With photocollage, Penny Siopsis has often used her own body as the "resting ground" for found objects and iconic artifacts important to South African history and society. Her work is very involved with the life of women, their identity and place in South African culture. In this piece, *My Lovely Day*, she uses video from home movies and layers of sound track to interweave her personal history with the lives of her mother and grandmother. The context for the video is a space reminiscent of one of South Africa's first small movie houses, the Metro Stop, owned by her grandfather in the 1930s. *My Lovely Day* has been described as "a collective endeavor: three generations of women collapsed into a moving narrative, three lifetimes folded into a day . . . . The voice of a woman sings the euphony of yesterday through the crackle of age and memory preserved in an old gramophone record . . . . It is the mother who holds the camera . . . Yet it is the grandmother who is perhaps most immediately 'visible,' who lends a word to the image from the grave . . . She speaks of travel, and blood ties, and belonging . . . We are reminded that the 'age of globalization' has extended well into the previous century; that travel and upheaval and relocation have always been part of tracing our position in the present . . . " (Jennifer Law, Johannesburg, 1997).

William Kentridge describes his six films chronicling the rise and fall of Soho Eckstein and Felix Teitlebaum as a "series of animated drawings for projection." Through a deceptively simple sequence of line drawings, which he layers and changes to create complex sequences of scenes, Kentridge creates a dense narrative about power, sexuality, wealth, race, and class. In the *History of the Main Complaint*, the sixth of the series, Kentridge says: "The film started as a sketch for an opera project scheduled for the next year, I needed to see whether it was possible to combine the technique of charcoal animation I use with the music of Monteverdi . . . and to see whether there was a rapport between the seventeenth century music and the very twentieth century systems of viewing the body --CAT scans, sonars, X-rays, magnetic resonance imaging, etc . . . The film was started at the time the TRC [Truth and Reconciliation Commission] was convened. The questions of guilt, responsibility, and collective memory that were in the air . . . made their way into the film . . . . The drawings start out as strictly subordinate to the needs of the film. But in the end the process turns in on itself and the film becomes an extraordinarily complicated and cumbersome machine for arriving at a set of drawings . . . "

This exhibition was co-curated for FotoFest by Linda Givon, Goodman Gallery, Johannesburg, South Africa and Eugenio Figueroa Valdés, independent curator in Havana, Cuba. Presentation of the exhibition was made possible by Fletcher Thorne-Thomsen, Jr., Vine Street Studios, and Linda Givon.

My Lovely Day, 1997
Penny Siopsis
Film Stills
(Courtesy of the Goodman Gallery, Johannesburg)

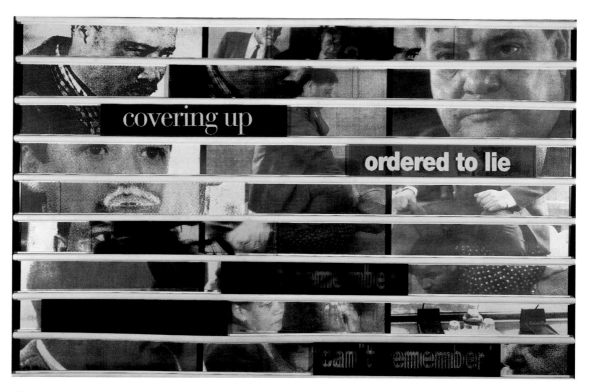

The Truth Games, 1997
Sue Williamson
Color Laser-prints, Wood, Perspex, Plastic
(Courtesy of the Goodman Gallery, Johannesburg)

History of the Main Complaint, 1989-1997
from SoHo Eckstein Films
William Kentridge
Drawings for Animated Films
(Courtesy of the Goodman Gallery,
Johannesburg)

If You Scratch, 1997
Pat Mautloa
Installation
(Courtesy of the Goodman
Gallery, Johannesburg)

Vanity At Frankies, 1997
Zwelethu Mthethwa
Installation, Detail From Drawer
Silver Gelatin Prints
(Courtesy of the Goodman Gallery,
Johannesburg)

Vanity At Frankies, 1997
Zwelethu Mthethwa
Installation
(Courtesy of the Goodman
Gallery, Johannesburg)

INFUSION

L'ubo Stacho

Over the past fifteen years, L'ubo Stacho's work has brought a special combination of photography, video, and installation to the history and context of Slovak art. It is an authentic outgrowth of his conceptual approach to art and incorporates a strong spiritual dimension, which has long been a leitmotif of Stacho's multifaceted creativity. Stacho's work moves away from the objective, classical character of documentary photography toward an exploration of the internal sources of creation, self-knowledge and self-expression, where humanism, spiritualism, and faith are the dominant characteristics.

In 1990, Stacho first presented the installation exhibited here. Titled *Infusion*, it contains his own self-portrait. In this piece, he deals with the problem or concept of artistically articulating or visualizing the sources of energy that emanate from objects and people as the essences of life's movement. The phenomenon of capturing these energies has become the center or axis of Stacho's later work. The idea of energy transfer(s) is developed and diversified by Stacho in a broad spectrum of work which incorporates the dimensions of classical photography with installations, happenings, the destruction of photography, and the transfer of the photographic image to cloth and canvas by means of monotypy.

In the series *Spiritual Journey*, Stacho uses photography more directly but creates diptychs that suggest other meanings and other worlds beyond the images themselves. He includes mixed-media works and a variety of non traditional materials to reflect the emanation of different kinds of life movements and the inner magic of life. In the diptychs, the juxtapositions of materials are placed in relationships that transform them into symbols and emblematic messages.

Dr. Alena Vrbanova (1994), edited by Lucia Benická

This exhibition is a site-specific installation commissioned for FotoFest. It is curated with Lucia Benická, independent curator and director of the House of Photography in Poprad, Slovakia. It has received assistance from the Trust for Mutual Understanding, the Ministry of Foreign Affairs in Slovakia, and the Embassy of Slovakia in the United States. Presentation of the exhibit has been made possible by Roy Murray, Wagon Works Building.

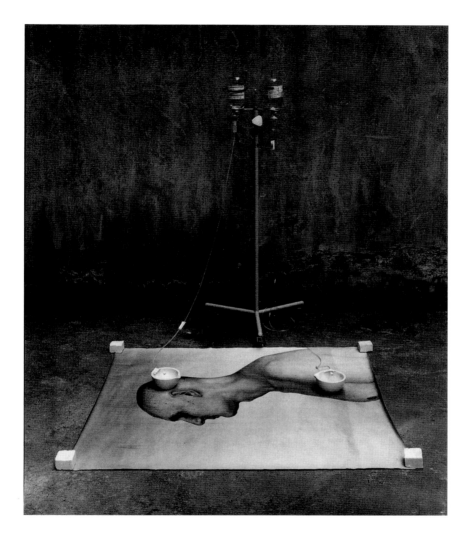

Infusion, 1990–1991
L'ubo Stacho
Mixed Media Installation

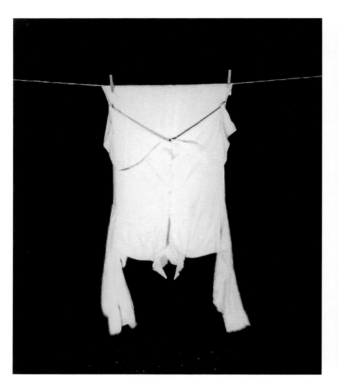 

Flower Depresion, 1991
from the cycle *Big Washing*, 1992
L'ubo Stacho
Diptych
Silver Gelatin Print, Monotype

Slovakia, 1991
L'ubo Stacho
Diptych
Silver Gelatin Print

WHITE LIGHTS

Harry Gruyaert

FOTOFEST EXHIBIT

OBSESSION

My style of photography might resemble scouting done for cinematography, but it is above all the result of an obsession, an obsession to repeat a powerful instant, the desire to relive it more intensely. This was how I worked in the beginning; today I tend more to spontaneously jump into my subject matter . . . to capture it immediately. . . .

COLOR

I believe that color is more physical, black and white more intellectual and abstract. In front of a black-and-white photo, you try more to understand what is happening between persons, whereas with color you should immediately be affected by the different tones that express a situation. So when many photographers used to working in black and white start shooting in color, they see an object which has a certain color. But the object and its color are one and the same thing, which by the way is one of the principles of the theory of perception. Form and color are inseparable. . . .
I place great importance on the quality of the prints. I see to it that the colors correspond as much as possible to my intentions. For me, a photograph exists when it "takes shape" as a print, when I can physically hold it in my hands, when my eye can wander over it and clearly distinguish the balance of proportions or the light. . . .

JUST A PICTURE

You could say I feel much closer to the plastic arts and to cinema than to "journalism." I have seen films where the images have taught me more than the color photos I knew at the time. For example, Red Desert by Antonioni. This was, by the way, the film for which he repainted entire streets in order to create a very precise atmosphere, which started me thinking. When I look at the work of photographers who stage their photos, I often say to myself that it would be much easier to paint the walls, like Antonioni, or ask people to wear something different. But I think that I would lose the miracle of the unexpected moment that takes your breath away, the very physical phenomenon of a photo that suddenly jumps out at you. On location, a real scuffle with reality goes on, and in a kind of trance, everything depends on capturing just one picture or perhaps missing everything. . . .

Harry Gruyaert
Excerpted by FotoFest from an interview by Brice Matthieussent in Gruyaert's book Morocco (1990).

This is the first presentation of the White Lights exhibition in the U.S. The exhibition was organized in conjunction with its copro-ducers, Magnum Photos and the Centre Nationale de la Photographie (CNP) in Paris. It was curated by former director of CNP Robert Delpire. The Houston installation was made possible by Dan Tidwell, and Jamie Mize, Treebeards Restaurant.

Ouarzalate, Morocco, 1985
Harry Gruyaert
(Courtesy of Magnum Photos)
Cibachrome Print

SPIRITS AND CONSTRUCTION

SWEENEY, COOMBS, AND FREDERICKS BUILDING
DOWNTOWN
MAIN STREET/MARKET SQUARE

ARTISTS: VICKI RAGAN, KATHLEEN CAMPBELL, CHARLES BIASINY-RIVERA

MEASURING THE INEFFABLE

My photos often reflect the tension between the unde-niable and the mysterious, or the improbable: history, autobiography, commerce, data, and "things" on the one hand, and myths, intuition, dreams, make-believe, and poetry on the other. For the last twenty years, I have been collecting and making things to assemble into dioramas, scenes of make-believe. Sometimes they are for the camera, sometimes for installation.

This body of work began as an exercise to construct environments out of maps and charts. It evolved into a more metaphorical exploration of the human need to make sense out of life and confront mortality through myth and rituals.

The photos piece together shards of information that are imbedded in our collective subconscious from arts and legends. They suggest the ambiguity of history and the differing interpretations of classical symbols.

The images in this exhibition are shot with outdated Polaroid positive-negative film. They seek to go beyond the mere ordering of facts by using an unpre-dictable medium to pull the imagery into the inexplic-able world of faith, instinct, and emotion.

Vicki Ragan
1997

North Pole, 1995
Vicki Ragan
Type C Print

ANGEL SERIES, OR PHOTOGRAPHS OF WIDELY-KNOWN NON-EXISTENT BEINGS

In this work, I am trying to touch on our society's embrace and rejection of nonrational phenomena. We live in a world threatened with extinction by the underlying irrationality of the human species, yet we cling to the vision of ourselves as scientific rationalists and the myth that we can comprehend and control ourselves and the forces of nature.

Several years ago, I had an idea to photograph "angels." I liked this idea precisely because it is impossible, even though everyone knows what an angel is or what they think it is. This series has evolved to include beings that are not "angels" and which have other messages. They might include the kinds of things we worship, things that we indulge ourselves in at the expense of others and the planet, or things that symbolize the biases hidden in our cultural assumptions.

Although the work is ironic in nature, even humorous at times, my intent is serious. In attempting to create an illusion of another, more spiritual reality, I try to suggest the void in which we are left because of our contemporary lack of faith. Thus, I try to insert an element of darkness in these images, perhaps as obvious as a snake or the more subtle shape of a flower. Also, each of these images is meant to be seen as "failed," unable to transcend its materiality. I paint or construct the backdrop of the image or use ordinary objects—bubble wrap, tape, coins, sheets, dime-store novelties, everyday clothing—to create a context referencing the spiritual tradition in Western art. I want the viewer to be aware of this contradictory juxtaposition and the artificiality of the image while, perhaps, being moved by it.

Charles Baudelaire once said: "We walk through a forest of symbols." By using symbols, I hope to touch on the conflicts between the universal longing for transcendence and the reality of our everyday lives. Heaven is always just outside our reach. We are grounded in a disappointing materialism forever hoping each illusion will lead us to spiritual truth.

Kathleen Campbell
1997

Angel of Technology, 1995
Kathleen Campbell
Hand Painted Silver Gelatin Print

MESSAGES

Messages is an ongoing body of photo-based work that deals with the suffering of the soul. These works are contemporary illuminations that offer solace and refuge, moments of meditation and comfort, for the worn psyche and tired spirit. I have recontextualized some of my early photographs to create vignetted scenes, each narrated by my own poetry. The original black-and-white photographs are bordered by colored sacred designs, and layers of pigments are used to build up the surface impressions. The seemingly irrational colors are in fact the colors of stained glass windows found throughout the regional churches of Italy.

The significance of *Messages* for me is that it creates a place where I can consider my purpose as an artist. From an early age, I have had an interest in religious and sacred art and its application towards fulfilling the spiritual needs of people. All through ancient history, art was used to illustrate the revelations and adoration inherent to the relationship between the spiritual world and terrestrial experience. Its purpose was to communicate the mysteries and myths that helped to inspire people. *Messages* is an attempt to revive that association and recall the earlier function of art. This work uses imagery from my Latino culture as a vehicle to embrace spiritual passion.

I have found references for this work in illuminated manuscripts, holy cards, and the Mexican retablo form. I use them not out of a desire to emulate them, but rather as a part of the comforting discovery that artists through all history have traveled the same pathways. This work has served to re-awaken my personal sense of spirituality and the sacred which had been diminished by the onslaught of rational thought. It is a process of restoring my sense of destiny. It is an effort to remind myself of my own fragile humanity.

Charles Biasiny-Rivera
1996

This exhibition has been made possible with the assistance of the Guadalupe Cultural Arts Center in San Antonio, Texas, and its artistic director, Kathy Vargas, as well as QRT Management Inc. and the historic Sweeney, Coombs, and Fredericks Building.

Messages From God, 1992
Charles Biasiny-Rivera
Photo Based Mixed Media with Text

BETWEEN PAST AND PRESENT

Contemporary Italian Photography and the New Landscape Experience

ARTISTS: OLIVO BARBIERI, GABRIELE BASILICO, VINCENZO CASTELLA, LUIGI GHIRRI, GUIDO GUIDI

Italy's last fifty years of economic development, along with the dominant social and cultural models that accompanied this development, have had a massive impact on the country's landscape. Modern architecture has spread throughout the country, even to old city centers, often resulting in paradoxical juxtapositions of past and present. Suburbs have grown extensively, transforming the land so much that post-World War II Italian artists have been obliged to find more adequate ways of representing the new scenery.

The stereotypical image of Italy as a romantic and pastoral Arcadia fell apart definitively under the devasting impact of the war and then the abrupt process of modernization during the so-called "reconstruction" period afterwards. Starting from the immediate postwar years, writers and filmmakers such as Italo Calvino, Vasco Pratolini, Michelangelo Antonioni, Pier Paolo Pasolini, Federico Fellini, and Roberto Rossellini found the modern and squalid peripheries more suitable as a base for their stories than the old city centers. Within Italian photography, this change in the iconography of the landscape occurred much later, namely in the early 1980s, when a clearly recognizable, although very heterogeneous, "school" of Italian landscape photography emerged. Two important exhibitions have demarcated this phenomenon:

Viaggo in Italia (Voyage to Italy), an itinerant show curated by Luigi Ghirri in 1984, and Muri di Carta (Walls of Paper), curated by Arturo Carlo Quintavalle on the occasion of XLV Venice Biennial. This last show is generally considered to be the first historical and critical retrospective on the subject.

The work of Eugène Atget, Walker Evans, Robert Frank, and Lee Friedlander, along with the New Topographers' "Provisional" and "Marginal" landscapes, and Bernd and Hilla Becher, in specific cases, have had a considerable impact on Italian contemporary landscape photography. Italian sources such as the conceptual work of Luigi Ghirri and Franco Vaacari, as well as the nineteenth-century tradition of anonymous industrialized photography as practiced in Italy by the Fratelli Alinari (Alinari Brothers), played a crucial role in normalizing the anticelebratory approach to the landscape genre. This genre has been defined by critic Claudio Marra as the "subversive normality of the gaze."

Olivo Barbieri, Gabriele Basilico, Vincenzo Castella, Luigi Ghirri, and Guido Guidi are now internationally known artists. They are all crucial figures within the context of Italian contemporary landscape photography. They are among the artists who turned their attention away from the classical sites of Italian monumental iconography to look at the more modern aspect of the country's urban development. They have all

Roma, 1995
Olivo Barbieri
Type C Print

contributed to a series of extremely important topographic campaigns commissioned by local governments and aimed at a rereading of the Italian territory. Some of these campaigns are still in process.

Despite their very diversified production, these photographers share a rejection of the stereotypical Italian "postcard" landscape in favor of a common and ongoing investigation of the everyday experience of the margins and peripheries of society—a less known and utterly unmonumental Italy where the old and new mix, resulting in an often uncanny scenery.

Nicoletta Leonardi, 1997
Doctoral student of the Department of
Art History and Archaeology
Columbia University, New York City

This exhibition has been curated for FotoFest by Martino Marangoni, founding director of the Fondazione Studio Marangoni, a photographic center in Florence, Italy. Assistance has been given by Gruppo Riello Spa and One Allen Center.

Comacchio, Argine Agosta, 1984-1989
Luigi Ghirri
Type C Print

Marghera, 1993
Guido Guidi
Chromogenic Print

Napoli, Posillipo, 1985
Vincenzo Castella
Chromogenic Print

Milano, 1989
Gabriele Basilico
Silver Gelatin Print

THE MEMORY OF A CITY
LIMA, PERU

The Photography Studio of Eugène (Eugenio) Courret
1863-1935

The photographic archives of Eugène (Eugenio) Courret, which are the property of the National Library of Peru, comprise 57,000 glass plate negatives taken in Lima from 1863 to 1935. In January 1993, a research team under the direction of Jorge Deustua, photographer and president of the Peruvian Council of Photography, completed a vast project identifying, cataloguing, and restoring this archive.

Originally from Angoulême in the west of France, Eugène Courret arrived in Lima in 1860. Other members of his family had set up business in Lima in the late 1830s, when the Peruvian government was encouraging the immigration of entrepreneurs from abroad. As a lucrative market, Lima attracted many foreign photographers. After his arrival in Lima, Courret went to work for the large French photographic firm, Eugenio Manoury and Co. In 1865, he started his own studio, the Studio Fotografía Central E. Courret y Hermanos, with his brother.

It was a time when many people wanted to have their portraits taken as cartes-de-visite. Very quickly, Courret's photography was sought after by Lima society. His studio became the leading portrait studio of Lima and attracted all the prominent families of Lima and well-known figures of the political, social, and artistic life of the city. In addition to cartes-de-visite, Courret offered large albumen prints, stereo views of Lima, reproductions of paintings, and beautifully bound volumes of urban scenes and selected portraits.

Courret returned to France shortly before 1900 and left his studio in the hands of his assistant Adolphe Dubreuil, who was already working as a professional photographer. The studio kept its original name and operated successfully until 1935. When it closed, the studio was run by Paul and Rene Dubreuil. The employees of the studio inherited the original glass plates of Courret and his assistant as payment for debts that had accumulated. In 1987, their descendants sold the Courret Archives to the National Library of Peru.

The archive reveals Courret to be a master of the late nineteenth-century classical genre of portrait photography. He is one of the great portraitists of his time in Latin America. This exhibition of over eighty prints covers seventy years of life in Lima. The selection was made to give a vision of Peruvian society, its evolution, and its particular characteristics. During this period, the country went through a succession of political crises inherited from the Wars for Independence: conflicts with Spain in 1877 and with Chile in 1879-83. Beginning in the 1870s, the country prospered due to revenues from the exploitation of guano.

Courret was not only a portraitist, he was also a witness of his time: the daily events of life in Lima, the architectural transformation, and the people of the city. Lima had a very cosmopolitan population in the late nineteenth century, and Courret was interested in people from different walks of life, social classes, and ethnic groups.

space in the city. Concurrently, AlienNation Co. will create a website to document/upload the project onto the Internet. On March 21, the performance films will be broadcast on the World Wide Web via World Link (www.wl.net).

The contextualist performances confront the notions that public spaces are coherent, nonconflictual, universally accessible, and either removed from larger market and social forces or defined exclusively by predictable capitalist investment interests. In one sense, the film settings try to restructure our experience of the space, examining the ways in which dominant historical narratives or Houston/Texas myths are inscribed in public space and perceived by local residents as well as immigrant, non-western sensibilities. In another sense, through the "holograms" we ask which public and private spaces are represented in local history, how movement and development are experienced today, and how the downtown workers, constructors, and independent artists envision their own projects in relation to civic myths of growth and urban development.

Our temporary and evolving installation does not try to create permanent artwork, but rather work that, by its presence, calls attention to movement, exchange, absence, dissolution, reappearance, fiction, and montage. It will highlight gaps without presuming to heal them, drawing attention to the underacknowledged role of the arts as a resource for the city's future.

Finally, the integrated project functions as a parachute, an unpredictable flight and fall into space. Our dance of the parachute explores how people and corporate bodies reinvent the city, as both an image and a physical space, thus creating a constant rhythm of deleting or reconverting. This cycle of decay and rebirth engineers histories, and our bodily performances, soundworks, and film projections will take place alongside the seemingly more concrete physical evidence of downtown urban redevelopment. Parachute will mark a space on the side of Main Street that momentarily occupies the gaps in Houston's civic mythology of progress.

The exact times of the excursions and performances during the first week of FotoFest will be announced through fliers and the local media and radio stations.

Members of AlienNation Co. include Elba Banos, Johannes Birringer, Tonya Borisov, Tania Botelho, Donald Calledare, Yiannis Efstathiou, Diana Glandt, Clarissa Guidry, Abdel Hernández, Jeongwon Joe, Zita Giraldo Lang, Malcolm Munro, Steve Paré, María de los Angeles Romero, Lorrie Spencer, and Hans Staartjes.

Johannes Birringer

These site-specific performances and installations, as well as the structural and logistical support needed to create the performance sets, received support from the Downtown District, the Downtown Historic District, and the City of Houston. Particular appreciation is due to the many individuals, building owners, and workers who generously cooperated in these ventures, especially to Alan J. Atkinson (The Americas), Blake Cordish (Bayou Place) and Jim Pirtle (316 Main Street) for offering their buildings as sites for the film set/installations.

THE FOTOFENCE

Now in its seventh year, the FotoFence is the annual exhibition of photographs and essays produced by students in FotoFest's Literacy Through Photography program. Throughout a yearlong curriculum, students photograph themselves, their families, their communities, and their dreams. After writing an essay to accompany each photographic assignment, the students design a poster combining text and image for public display. Their work provides visions and versions of life in southeast Texas that are revelatory, intimate, and beautiful. The FotoFence has been displayed in the George R. Brown Convention Center, the Magnolia Multi Service Center, the Marathon Oil building, and the Pennzoil building. FotoFest 98 is the third year for the FotoFence in the lobby of the NationsBank Center. There are nine Houston Independent School District schools represented in the exhibition.

David Brown
Director, Literacy Through Photography
FotoFest

The FotoFence and Literacy Through Photography program have received special support from Fuji Photo Film USA, CANON USA Inc., Fuji Color Processing, Houston Endowment Inc., William Stamps Farish Foundation, Favrot Fund, Powell Foundation, Harris and Eliza Kempner Fund, and the City of Houston and the Texas Commission on the Arts through the Cultural Arts Council of Houston/Harris County.

FotoFence, FotoFest 1994
Wendy Watriss
George R. Brown Convention Center
Color Transparency

FOTOFEST COLLABORATIONS

FOTOFEST

2

COLLABORATIONS

DANNY TISDALE

An Artist For A Change

A COLLABORATION BETWEEN
FOTOFEST AND PROJECT ROW HOUSES

We'd already begun working with artist Danny Tisdale when we received a letter from him. Danny had decided he no longer wanted to be considered an artist, that among other things, he was tired of not being able to have the people he grew up with appreciate his work, and that he wanted to address a world bigger than the art world. So he decided to move his work, which previously had addressed issues of "race" and identity, more directly into the sphere of politics.

Will R. Wilkins, Real Art Ways, Hartford, Connecticut, 1995

In a series of city-to-city public installations, Tisdale has used the model of the political election process to fashion a movable campaign headquarters from which to launch his "Arts Platform" for Community Change. From this interactive venue the public can gather and learn firsthand about his "campaign" [New York City Council] complete with voter registration information, promotional material, computers with links to the Internet, televisions tuned to C-Span, video monitors, and cameras standing ready to tape interviews with the visitors. Within the installation, the artist also provides a series of captioned photographs making what he calls *The Journey Series*, which utilizes the artist's own life and guiding principles in his journey for change . . .

Jeffrey Hoone, Light Work, Syracuse, New York, 1996

Danny Tisdale: An Artist For A Change is a community-based project dedicated to fulfilling an ongoing mission of advocating, presenting, and creating multidisciplinary art collaborations through performances, exhibitions, residencies, workshops, Street/Forums, and educational and mentoring projects. Participants in the project have included youth, students, artists, residents, administrators, organizations, city officials, and citizens interested in telling their stories and speaking about community experience. The *Danny Tisdale: An Artist For A Change* project was created in 1995 as a collaborative program seeking to cross traditional and untraditional boundaries between artistic disciplines and the public, generating cooperative projects between individuals, communities, and organizations leading to change as we enter into the twenty-first century. The project is designed to raise awareness of contemporary art and life beyond traditional visual and performance art constituencies and create partnerships between theaters, visual arts institutions, community-based organizations, schools, colleges, local business, and civic groups. The Houston project is a collaboration between FotoFest, Project Row Houses, citizens of the Third Ward, and local organizations involved in the arts and civic affairs.

Danny Tisdale, Los Angeles, 1997

This exhibition is presented by AT&T, with special support from Project Row Houses, Margaret Cullinan Wray Charitable Lead Annuity Trust, and the Lombard/Freid Gallery in New York.

"... art to be more than art...a social art " Joseph Beuys

photo by Renee Cox
and Danny Tisdale
Color Transparency

José, student from the south Bronx. Still from video response workshop at Bronx Museum in New York. Jose was concerned with education and the violence happening in his community. Videographer was Austin Phillips.

Minareen, resident and assistant director at the Upper Albany Neighborhood Collaborative (UANC), Hartford, Ct. Still from video response workshop in Hartford. Minareen was concerned that the community needed to be more involved in neighborhood decision-making by political officials.

Ella, Hartford Ct. resident. Still from video response workshop in Hartford. Ella was concerned with "the conversation and disrespect from area youth, local unemployment rate and non-voters who live in Hartford."

Photos by Danny Tisdale

Hartford Campaign Headquarters, *Danny Tisdale Artist For A Change*. Hartford, Ct., 1995. First campaign headquarters at Upper Albany Neighborhood Collaborative (UANC) in collaboration with Real Art Ways (RAW) and the Community Redevelopment Association (CRA). Headquarters had video monitors on porch, campaign banner, mailer and voter posters. This project included a community Town Hall meeting, workshops for change on business, education, and art, and a creative writing book with high school students. Photo by Danny Tisdale

Danny Tisdale, Delegate for the
Independence Party. April 1996,
New York City, Self-portrait taken
at New York City Independence
Party Convention for Assembly
District #70 in Harlem. Tisdale and
running mate Jamie Richardson
were the first New York State
Committee Seal Representatives
for the Independence Party, one
of the first steps in building the
Independence Party. Party advisor
Fred Newman is in the background.
Photo by Danny Tisdale, from
The Journey Series.

UNIVERSAL ART PLATFORM
DANNY TISDALE: AN ARTIST FOR CHANGE

1. Elect community legislators.
2. Environmentally safe materials and products.
3. Economic investment and tax incentives.
4. Community decision-making.
5. Join community and school boards.
6. Promote legislator collaborations.
7. Legislator term limits.
8. Less government in our personal and private lives.
9. Freedom of expression and speech.
10. No identity politics or actions for a specific group.

EUSTÁQUIO NEVES

FOTOFEST COLLABORATION

"My project on Urban Chaos began life independently of the construction of images. I started Urban Chaos based on the social inequalities that exist in Brazil and on the proliferation of signs within my culture. In developing this project, I chose the region of Contagem. It still has active polluting factories while others lie in ruins. A dead river separates the factories from a shanty town. [It] reminds me of a place that Caetano Veloso describes in one of his songs: 'Everything here looks in ruins, as though it is still being built.' . . . My experiments with constructed images also take all of this into account."

Eustáquio Neves, 1996-1997

"From the project of Urban Chaos . . . I moved on to find out more about the Arturos community in the same district where I also used to live. The members of this centenary community are direct descendants of Arthur Camilo, who died in 1956, aged seventy-six, and whose life was strongly influenced by being the son of parents who were slaves. The unshaken structure of this group stems from their spiritual life, self-respect, discipline, and faith. My first contact with the Arturos was during one of their religious celebrations. In these festivities, the sound of each drum, the dancing and singing, and each object has its own meaning.
My work is conceptualized from the relevance of these signs; beyond and above any record, I want to show with it my emotion and the mystical significance of things . . ."

Eustáquio Neves, 1996-1997

The text has been excerpted by FotoFest from the catalogue Eustáquio Neves, Monograph, by Autograph (London, 1997), and the book Novas Travessias: Contemporary Brazilian Photography, by Maria Luiza Melo Caravalho (London, 1996).

This exhibition was developed at NAFOTO 1997, the Month of Photography in São Paulo, Brazil, with assistance from photographer Lily Sverner.

Arturos, 1994
Eustáquio Neves
Mixed Media

GARY HILL

Reflex Chamber

Installation for Rice University Art Gallery

Gary Hill's sculptures and large-scale installations make inventive use of new photographic and video technologies. Several themes thread through these works. Hill often explores the nature of perception; he also investigates liminal or in-between spaces among artist, work of art and viewer, or among body, mind, and machine. As curator Chris Beuce has noted, in "a medium (video) that is particularly fluid, Hill works toward subjects (meaning, consciousness) that are elusive, in a way that seems as basic and mysterious as the way an object enters the eye and becomes cognitive thought."

A contemplative ambiance characterized many of Hill's early pieces, but his most recent works use strobe lights to elicit a strong visceral response. Hill uses this tactic in *Reflex Chamber*, an installation presented by the Rice University Art Gallery. A chamber sits inside the gallery, and within this darkened room, a series of video projections bounce from a mirror to a tabletop; this process partially replicates the workings of a camera or a human eye. Flashes of light disrupt the images while Hill speaks texts that have been digitally altered — compressed at some points, stretched at others — so that they can only be understood intermittently. The Rice Gallery's presentation of *Reflex Chamber* marks Hill's first solo exhibition in Houston and allows audiences familiar with the seminal work *Tall Ships*, 1992 (which was in Houston as part of a recent touring exhibition) to witness the most recent developments in Hill's work.

Stephanie Smith

Reflex Chamber, 1996
Gary Hill
Single-channel video/sound installation
(Courtesy Donald Young Gallery, Seattle)

RE-IMAGINING VIETNAM

ARTISTS: AN-MY LÊ, CRAIG J. BARBER, TIMOTHY P. KARR, ABBY ROBINSON

In our past FotoFest exhibitions, Houston Community College Central has chosen photographers whose images reflected the cultures of our student body. Central College and the Midtown area serve a large Vietnamese population as well as veterans from the war. This year we chose photographers to represent these students and neighbors, and to show the rest of us some images of the country from which they came. This exhibition includes a Vietnamese photographer who returned home after living in the U.S.; a veteran of the Vietnam War who returned to take photographs; an American who was awarded a grant to visit Vietnam and photograph the country; and an American who worked there for several years.

Michael Golden
Houston Community College Central

AN-MY LÊ

In 1975, at age fifteen, I fled from the war in Vietnam with my family and resettled in the United States. In 1994, I returned for the first time and began making a series of photographs that are informed by my memories of growing up in southern Vietnam and my family's stories and perceptions of northern Vietnam. My photographs portray a traditional culture inextricably bound to the land while confronting the realities of modern-day Vietnam.

CRAIG J. BARBER

How does one condense intense memories and emotions into a brief statement? Life was intense in 1967, and it was equally intense in 1995. These images are the images of Vietnam through my 1995 eyes, the same eyes that witnessed far too much in 1967 but were eager to look again eighteen years later. On March 15, 1995, I made the following entry in my journal:

Hoi An, Viet Nam

The lack of discernible change is jarring at times. More than once as I have wandered the small hamlets searching for images, I have felt on patrol. The weight of my pack feeling all too familiar and the tripod feeling like a weapon. I am not in the midst of flashbacks, I am in complete control of my faculties, yet déjà vu runs deep in my veins while winding my way along narrow dirt paths and bamboo groves, scattered hooches and barking dogs, water buffalo and rice paddies, fishing villages and coconut trees. It would be impossible not to remember events. These moments are disconcerting. I did not brush them aside.

TIMOTHY P. KARR

The layers of cultural sediment that make up our images of Hanoi weigh so heavily on our understanding of the city that it can hardly be viewed in any other light. But beneath these cutout portraits lurks another Vietnam, one difficult and shaded gray, one overlooked since it takes too long to explain. I decided to piece together a portrayal of Hanoi that looks beyond the simple history to reveal manifold complexities of a place.

I moved to Hanoi in 1993 and began photographing the city just as new economic reforms began to take hold. Communist Vietnam had abandoned its rigid postwar regimen in a new experiment with market forces, dubbed "doi moi" by the Party. . . For many citizens, the changes represented an opportunity to open up businesses, get rich, and build up a new life for one's family. As a photographer, I turned my attention to Hanoi under this "doi moi"—its coming out into the world, and what the Vietnamese describe as "doi thuong," or daily life.

ABBY ROBINSON

I grew up knowing about Vietnam. I wanted to see it after the war; I was interested to see what images could be made after the war. I am fascinated by the way the camera turns the ordinary into the extraordinary, how fluidly it turns the everyday into the unexpected. While I often go to foreign countries to shoot, the pictures themselves are of quite ordinary places.

Through my exposure to Vietnam and the work of its photographers, my own pictures acquired a reserve and lushness. I learned how to use color in Vietnam. Vietnamese photographers explore beauty, in the landscape and in daily life, with gentleness and a distinctive sense of place. However, my subject matter and the way I use color are very different from that of my Vietnamese counterparts, and I deal with aspects of life that Vietnamese photographers don't document.

The exhibition is presented by AT&T with additional support by the Asian Cultural Council. This exhibition has been organized by FotoFest in collaboration with the Art Department of Houston Community College Central Campus. Special acknowledgment goes to Michael Golden, Chair of the Art Department, who has coordinated the exhibition at HCC. In Hanoi, assistance was provided by David Thomas, founder of the Indochina Arts Project.

Sapa, 1995
Abby Robinson
Cibachrome Print

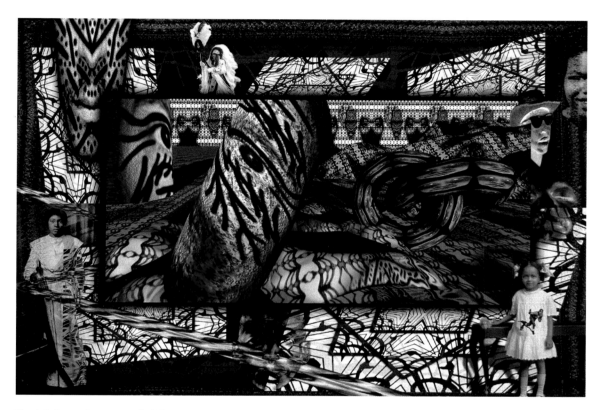

Untitled, from the series, *Soul Searching*, 1997
Stephen Marc
Digital Montage and Ilfochrome Print

FRANK MARTIN

Retrospective

I think of my medium as photographic monoprints instead of photography. This underlines the difference between my work and conventional photographs. Conventional photography is strongly dependent on what's in front of the camera. In conventional photography, identical multiple prints can be produced from the same negative. My work is shaped and dominated by the work I do in the lab.

The prints are made on a German fiber paper treated in a modified archival process to ensure that their permanence is equal to or better than other museum-quality photographs.

The camera I use is a 4x5 view camera in which I use a recently introduced black-and-white technical film originally developed for use in electron microscopes.

Because this film is so sharp and grain free, the print size—about four by five and a half feet—is limited only by the size of the largest photo paper I've been able to find.

Each piece is one of a kind, created by my working on the surface of the print with a variety of photo chemicals, artist's brushes, sponges, and, when the mood strikes, some freehand sloshing and smearing.

After midnight in Texas, listening to Bach's Mass in B Minor, I learned how to break the rules, what to throw away, and what to keep.

Frank Martin, 1942-1994

Force Lifeforce, 1989
Frank Martin
Photographic Monotype
(Courtesy of Collection of Walter Hopps)

MUSEUMS/NONPROFIT ART SPACES

MUSEUM

3

NONPROFIT

ART SPACES

MUSEUM OF FINE ARTS, HOUSTON

Years Ending in Nine

Whether turning to a new decade or a new century, we use years ending in nine to reflect on the past and speculate about the future. Selected from the collection of the Museum of Fine Arts, Houston, *Years Ending in Nine* features photographs made the last year of each decade between 1899 and 1989. Pieces may crystallize an issue of the prior decade or anticipate a prevailing concern in the next decade. The exhibition features aesthetic movements ranging from Pictorialism to Modernism, and from Documentary to Post-Modern representations. It includes pictures originally made for the printed page, such as *Life* and *Vogue*, and large installation pieces composed of many photographs.

The exhibition is not intended to be a thorough survey of photography in this century, but to highlight aesthetic issues as particularly illuminated by Houston's collection. The museum's greatest strengths are European and American works made between the World Wars, and photographs made in the United States after 1945. The exhibition reflects those strengths. From the period between the wars, there are photographs by Manuel Alvárez Bravo, Brassaï,

Walker Evans, Jaromir Funke, Sidney Grossman, André Kertesz, Tina Modotti, Laszlo Moholy-Nagy, Paul Strand, and Edward Weston. The selections also indicate the museum's great depth in the holdings of certain individual artists, who will be represented in more than one decade. Among the artists who came to prominence after World War II, the exhibition includes the works of Aaron Siskind, Harry Callahan, Minor White, Roy DeCarava, W. Eugene Smith, Robert Frank, Irving Penn, Josef Sudek, Diane Arbus, Lee Friedlander, Ray K. Metzker, Joel Sternfeld, Esther Parada, and Cindy Sherman.

Anne Tucker

Past Recovery, 1979
Esther Parada
100 hand-toned silver gelatin photographs
displayed in rows of ten
Target Collection of American Photography

GLASSELL SCHOOL OF ART

Classical Sensibilities:
Images by Alain Gerard Clement and George Dureau

Flesh and Guns, 1996
George Dureau
Silver Gelatin Print

The exhibition *Classical Sensibilities: Images by Alain Gerard Clement and George Dureau* relates the work of two contemporary photographers that at first glance may not appear to be interconnected, but in fact is connected through the artists' classical acumen.

Houstonian Alain Gerard Clement has created and photographed surrealistic visions that are emotionally charged and strongly influenced by European traditions and classical themes. Clement utilizes the photogenic process. It is a "cameraless" process using light-sensitive paper and natural sunlight. A strong sense of religious content resonates throughout Clement's imagery and installations.

George Dureau made his photographs in the late 1970s — male nudes, the dwarfs, and the physically challenged inhabitants of New Orleans' French Quarter. The photographs initially look odd and voyeuristic, yet they possess a classical dignity. He creates a stateliness and beauty where one might see only their deformity and feel pity. Dureau's devout concern for these individuals is equal to the depth of Clement's spirituality.

Valerie Loupe Olsen
Administrative Dean, Glassell School of Art
Museum of Fine Arts, Houston

The exhibition Classical Sensibilities: Images by Alain Gerard Clement and George Dureau was curated by Valerie Loupe Olsen, Administrative Dean of the Glassell School of Art, The Museum of Fine Arts, Houston.

Lucretia, 1997
Alain Gerard Clement
Photogenic Print

MUSEUM OF HEALTH & MEDICAL SCIENCE

Microcosm: Views of Microscopic Forms

Microcosm: Where Science Meets Art

The incredibly detailed photographs in the exhibition, *Microcosm: Views of Microscopic Forms,* are taken through the lens of a scanning electron microscope. These photomicrographs reveal the remarkable detail and intricate beauty present in a world that exists beyond human perception.

A scanning electron microscope (SEM) allows images to be magnified up to 200,000 times. With the SEM, one can look at a whole object, such as an insect, or at a small part of a larger object. To get the best image, most specimens must be coated with a very thin layer of metal (usually gold) to make them electrically conductive.

Electron photomicrographs are always originally black-and-white images because electrons, unlike light waves, do not provide information about a specimen's coloring. The photos can be artificially colored later to help distinguish between different structures in a specimen.

A jury of scientists and artists selected the exhibit's sixty works on the basis of their artistic composition, originality, tonal balance, and photographic quality.

The exhibition includes works from the following photomicrographers: Steve Brocco, William Carty, Richard Cloney, Dale Cunningham, Michael Davidson, Mike Eng, Douglas Keene, Susan Kent, Dennis Kunkel, Norma Lang, Daniel Luchtel, Scott MacLaren, Rodman Miller, Barbara Reine, Ed Rubel, Eric Schabtach, Elaine Simons, Carla Stehr, and Kenneth Tiekotter.

Cindy Bandemer

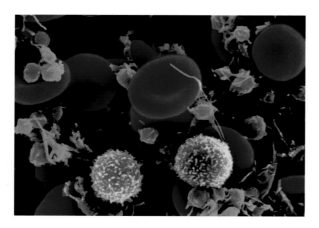

Human red blood cell, platelets and T-lymphocites, n/d
Denis Kunkel
Scanning electron photomicrograph
with colorization/19,200x magnification

GALVESTON ARTS CENTER

Keith Carter — Photographs: Twenty-five Years

Keith Carter's photographs linger in the mind like images from an almost-remembered dream. Evocative and haunting, they capture what Carter calls the "little askew moments" that allow viewers to see beyond the surface reality.

Keith Carter-Photographs: Twenty-five Years is a survey of his work from 1973 to the present. The exhibition brings together 80 photographs chosen to represent the range and development of his work. Drawing inspiration from popular culture, religion, folklore, stories, travels, and Carter's own East Texas roots, the photographs testify to the beauty, mystery, and deep abiding grace woven into our daily lives.

Keith Carter is the Walles Chair Professor of Art at Lamar University, Beaumont. This exhibition was organized by the Wittliff Gallery of Southwestern and Mexican Photography at Southwest Texas State University, San Marcos, from its permanent collection. It celebrates the publication by the University of Texas Press of *Keith Carter-Photographs: Twenty-fiveYears*, Carter's sixth book since 1988.

Clint Willour

"I photograph ghosts. Mostly they are my own, sometimes they belong to others."

Keith Carter

Giant, 1997
Keith Carter
Toned Silver Gelatin Print

DIVERSEWORKS ARTSPACE

Stories about Us: Photographs from Juárez

This exhibition of more than fifty color prints by Javier Aguilar, Jaime Bailleres, Julían Cardona, Gabriel Cardona, Alfredo Carrillo, Ramiro Escobar, Raúl Lodoza, Jaime Murrieta, Miguel Perea, Margarita Reyes, Ernesto Rodríguez, Manuel Sáenz, Lucio Espino, Aurelio Suárez Nuñez, and Carlos Vigueras presents an eye-opening view of life in Juárez, a city situated at the confluence of powerful social and economic forces found on the border between Mexico and the United States.

Separated only by a river, the Río Grande, the more than 2 million inhabitants of Juárez, Chihuahua, and El Paso, Texas constitute one of the world's largest border communities. With a thirty-year history of economic exploitation and unregulated growth, the Juárez/El Paso community is a model of what the world may increasingly resemble under the new global economy, a world in which powerful industrial states transform the cultural landscape of the underdeveloped nations they tap for cheap labor. The uncompromising work of these photographers documents the conditions in Juárez, confronting the viewer with images that governments and economists often prefer not to acknowledge. By exploding fairy tale depictions of life in Juárez, they demand that viewers consider both the true price of free trade and our collective future as residents of a border region in flux.

Here, squatters in outlying shantytowns are electrocuted as they jack into city power lines for pirated electricity, and teenage girls disappear during their pre-dawn walks to the *maquiladoras*, foreign-owned factories built to take advantage of low labor costs and lax or unenforced environmental regulations. The girls are often found—raped and murdered—in the sand outside the city. Other photographs offer surprising insights into the nature of survival in this economic frontier town: kindergarten students playing in the shadow of a towering industrial smokestack or a ritual drummer's ecstatic dance in the public square.

Most of the featured artists are staff photographers for *Diaro de Juárez,* the city's leading daily newspaper. Working with old Pentax cameras and the paper's daily ration of one roll of film, they comb the streets in search of images. Asked why they live in Juárez or why they have chosen this difficult, sometimes dangerous subject, several of these photographers answered simply, "I see things here that I can't see anywhere else." The exhibition at DiverseWorks Artspace will be the first in the United States—the first chance for a U.S. audience to see the city through their eyes, to explore the depth within their seemingly innocuous words.

DiverseWorks Artspace will publish a catalogue in conjunction with the exhibition with a statement by the exhibition curator William Tuman. The show will be accompanied by a hardcover book, *The Laboratory of Our Future* (136 pages, 100 color prints) by Aperture.

William Tuman, Exhibition Curator

Untitled, 1994
Jaime Bailleres
Cibachrome Print

GOETHE INSTITUT—HOUSTON

AfterImages from America: Kai-Olaf Hesse

Presented in conjunction with the Houston Center for Photography

This exhibition deals with the specific American visual landscapes of politics, industry, science, and movies, while referring to American history in general. This subjective and personal survey presents American spaces defined by major cultural products as their places of origin.

These themes can also be looked at as product—major inventions, economic developments, and major cultural phenomena that changed the 20th century. In the four cities represented—Washington, D.C., Detroit, Los Alamos, and Los Angeles—a very specific product materialized as a mixture of part American dream, part American history, and part American ingenuity.

This process of development shaped each of these cities in a distinctive, visible, and unique way. Not only did the names of these products become synonymous with their cities, but the visual character of each city reveals the process of the creation of its particular cultural product.

AfterImages suggests visual, commercial, and semiotic links among four entirely different products and geographies within the American experience, while tracking the shifts of meaning and the changing use of symbols, icons, and American emblems.

Untitled, 1997
Kai-Olaf Hesse

FARISH GALLERY, RICE UNIVERSITY SCHOOL OF ARCHITECTURE

Houston: Mundane & Otherwise Images by Craig McCormick and Ben Thorne

Employing different means and methods, both series of photographs attempt to record and create real yet conceptual interior spaces.

Craig McCormick's photographs of Allen Parkway Village capture the subtly complex spatial qualities which resulted from the closure and subsequent partial demolition of the social housing complex. The surfaces of the remaining interiors retain colors, textures and patterns which accumulated over the life of the building. The removal of interior walls allowed the ceilings and floors of the divided space to be seen as one continuous spatial whole, allowing a view through the building that had been unattainable since its construction. The composition within the images varies only slightly throughout the series, each objectively record the newly revealed depth of space within the building, capturing the essential character of the spaces.

The photographs by Ben Thorne are of small models which create images suggestive of full scale interiors. The wall, ceiling, and floor surfaces are used to create and manipulate a spatial reading so that the physical location of the planes relative to one another is not apparent. The distinction between the architecture and the landscape is blurred through the reflectivity of the surfaces. The figure is one of the elements which activates the images, instigating a dynamic and suggesting a narrative.

One project exists conceptually, creating images of spaces through controlled use of surface planes and the human scale, thriving toward specificity and concreteness. The other exists in the recording of built spaces which exist relative to a specific time, nature, sociopolitical direction, and essence, yet moves toward the realm of the abstract. It is here that we find a common meeting place in the space of the image.

Untitled #07, 1997
Ben Thorne
Cibachrome Print

Allen Parkway Village, 1997
Craig McCormick
Cibachrome Print

HOUSTON CENTER FOR PHOTOGRAPHY

Cameraeye Voyeurage: George Peters, Melanie Walker

When light enters a space within a darkened room or through the pinpoint aperture of a camera, something magical happens. The dark is transformed into an upside-down theater of light. These little machines spend much of their time sleeping, with lens caps covering their eyes and shutter curtains closing their stages. When our cameras enter the realm of sleep long enough to create a dream dynamic, the faint light starts to develop scenes quite different from what the photographer sees through the series of complex lenses and shutters. Recollections of memories flash through the consciousness of the black box cameras—blending to form an extensive panoramic memory of each camera's unique experiences.

This interactive installation features an array of different puppet and slide theater camera viewing boxes set on tripod legs within the gallery space. They are posed gazing at various tableaux set up on the walls, the ceiling, and the floor of the gallery. By looking into the viewfinders, the scenes will be transformed, some by subtle means and others by extraordinary visual shifts into the realm of the camera eye dreamtime.

The voyage of the camera eye in this story leads us to landscapes of familiar places in our visual memory, but with another sense in place. The Cameraeye is our visual warrior sent on a voyage to see where no one has seen before.

Untitled, n/d
Melanie Walker and George Peters
Installation Illustration

Invented Landscapes: Images by Carlos Díaz
Gallery X, Houston Center for Photography

"Photographs are curious things. They resonate in a space somewhere between that which we perceive to be fact and that which is not. This dichotomy between fact and fiction is essential in my work."

Carlos Díaz

The images in *Invented Landscapes* utilize the amusement park environment of Coney Island, New York as their base. Steel-plate engravings taken from nineteenth-century patent and engineering journals are collaged onto gelatin silver photographs. Rather than rely solely on an optical rendering of literal objects in a real space, these images are "physically sculpted" using incompatible subject matter to reference a literal reality. The results are literal records of fictional space or invented landscapes constructed of wood and brick and steel . . . or they can be both. The parts and pieces are taken from highly detailed renderings of mechanical inventions that relate primarily to manufacturing, mining, farming, and transportation. The relationship between these inventions and the Coney Island landscape is significant in that the prosperity resulting from the Industrial Revolution made possible the time for leisure and amusement. The collage then is one that merges the "Coney Island of the mind" with that of cold, hard steel. It is a fusion of the functional forms of labor with the fun and fantasy of the carnival —one finite, the other infinite.

Invented Landscape #20-NY, n/d
Carlos Diaz
Collage, Steel Engravings
on Silver Gelatin Print

C. G. JUNG EDUCATIONAL CENTER

Fugitive Visions/A Garden Series
Images by Shirli Marcantel

There is a mystic reality that permeates some gardens, especially the old ones that have felt the hands of generations of caretakers. Alone in such a place, one can almost hear the faint whispers of people and times past.

Gardens hold fugitive visions of life and death, of effortless beauty, and unruly struggle. They are metaphors and mirrors of the lives that have created them, cared for them, or abandoned them. It is signif-icant that in all cultures, paradise is understood to be a beautiful garden.

I feel that photography is the most poetic medium to capture the essence of a garden.

These images document certain gardens and the forms within them, that have called to my imagination. They are rich with untold stories and secret realities created by human hands, time and natural processes.

Shirli Marcantel

Untitled from *Fugitive Visions /
A Garden Series*, n/d
Shirli Marcantel
Selenium Toned
Silver Gelatin Print

Untitled from *Fugitive Visions / A Garden Series,* n/d
Shirli Marcantel
Selenium Toned Silver Gelatin Print

Untitled from *Fugitive Visions / A Garden Series*, n/d
Shirli Marcantel
Selenium Toned Silver Gelatin Print

Untitled from *Fugitive Visions / A Garden Series*, n/d
Shirli Marcantel
Selenium Toned Silver Gelatin Print

NORTH HARRIS COMMUNITY COLLEGE

Physical Natures: Children Series
Images by Debra Rueb

My photographs are about the physical natures of children. I explore and record visually while they are exploring physically their own inherent tendencies and capabilities. My series consists of photographs taken from different events or activities of children. I photograph swim meets and taekwondo classes, as well as my own niece and nephew jumping on a trampoline. My work captures the controlled energy that is first found and then released in a calculated way with precise goals by my subjects. There is an exhilaration evident in the physical freedom of weightlessness and the mental challenge of competition children often exhibit in their activities and play. This ongoing project of documenting the activities and behaviors of children follows a long photographic tradition of capturing action on film.

Debra Rueb

Interlude, 1995
Debra Rueb
Silver Gelatin Print

Figure and Form
Images by Sean Porea

I drew inspiration from the human figure to create this series of insightful images using black-and-white infrared materials. My images tend to be of higher contrast than conventional black-and-white photographs. Infrared film produces very grainy pictures, giving the feeling of an impressionistic painting, with a continuity to tonal skin values and dark backgrounds. All of the subjects I photograph are nude and both genders are equally represented in the series. I photograph my subjects, from a diverse racial background, without props. Thus, the images direct the viewer to the actual shape and form. Rarely is the entire body seen and faces are obscured. The human figure thus photographed is presented as graceful and powerful and gives the viewer a greater understanding of the marvelous works of art each figure represents.

Sean Porea

Infrared nude #2, 1995
Sean Porea
Silver Gelatin Print

RICE UNIVERSITY MEDIA CENTER

Keep on Rolling: My Years with the Skateboarders of Houston, Texas
Jesse DeMartino

When I first began this project almost three years ago, my primary motivation was to provide a visual alternative to the magazines of the skateboarding industry. As a teenager, I had read these magazines religiously, looking up to the professional skaters as idols and treating their statements as gospel. I found them incredibly eye-catching and subsequently plastered my walls with them. After studying photography at college, however, I began to find such photos overly glitzy and slick. Lit with multiple flashes made with fisheye lenses and hyper-saturated film, these images had an artificial studiolike quality. Such photos rank high in surface drama, but do not stimulate deeper interest.

I wanted to change all that and put spontaneity and realism into these photographs by documenting every aspect of skateboarder life in an utterly straight and objective manner. I had been a skateboarder for over ten years. After all, I was an insider making images of my own subculture, not some anthropologist from the outside doing a visual study. A few months into the project, I decided to stop jumping from one group of skateboarders to another and photograph the cluster I related to best, the ones I considered my friends.

By concentrating on a small group, I could profoundly and candidly reveal the skateboarding subculture and how it relates to the reality of the broader culture. In my images, one can see a number of issues that confront us daily: the need for comradeship, the frustra-tion of being part of a marginalized group ridiculed by society, the adolescent desire to feel unique and independent while conforming to the standards of a larger peer group, the freedom gained from participating in a sport without coaches and rules, the positive and negative effects of drug use, the perpetual harassment from police officers who see us as nothing more than a menace, and the willingness to take risks and push the boundaries of acceptable behavior. Bringing myself and my camera into the streets, the skate parks, the homes, the parties, I want to reveal what it truly means to be a member of this band of urban outcasts.

Those whom I photograph are my friends, people with whom I share my life experiences and innermost feelings. I am a participant as well as an observer. In this manner, my project moves into the realism of personal documentary, a genre used by Larry Clark and Nan Goldin, who frankly expose the gritty details of their own lives.

To complement my photographic work, I have been keeping a written journal for more than a year. This journal allows me to fully explore all the corridors of my skateboarding world. At times, it is strictly narrative storytelling. Other days, it is like I am writing my own memoirs as I turn inward and examine my own private thoughts and feelings about the people I photograph, my relationship to them as participant and observer, and memories of my own skateboarding experiences before I began photographing. At still other times, I play the role of ethnographic anthropologist, investigating the unique practices and rituals of skateboarders and their views on the ethics of documentary photography.

During the three years that I have been working on this project, I continually ask myself: *Does this body of images have enough cultural resonance to be truly important in some crucial way, or am I just wasting my time?* Each time I question the work, however, I ultimately decide to push forward, delving deeper and deeper into our subculture's complicated existence.

Jesse DeMartino

Phillip, Nate, Martin, & Wayne,
Downtown Houston, 1996
Jesse DeMartino
Silver Gelatin Print

O'KANE GALLERY
UNIVERSITY OF HOUSTON DOWNTOWN

The "I" of Downtown
Images by Vivian Lee

The project and exhibition of *The "I" of Downtown* explores the art-making process and reflects on how people see themselves in relation to downtown Houston. This city in search of an identity seems to be constantly reinventing itself. It is a city of great architectural interest, including well-sited sculpture by regional and world-renowned artists. Downtown has experienced peaks and valleys of growth and currently seems to be experiencing community redevelopment as a people-friendly city.

Thirty participants of diverse backgrounds, plus two professional photographers, are contributing to make up the exhibition. Student participants were selected from Marshall Middle School and Jeff Davis High School by Jennifer Hightower, director of the UHD Educational Talent Search Program, Upward Bound. Marie Jones and Eileen Brown of Foley's Oasis program assisted in contacting the senior citizens.

My intent was to involve a broadly representative spectrum of the community in a photographic integration of downtown Houston, old and new. The process consisted of two workshops that took participants on a downtown walking tour. Each was given a scavenger-hunt list with suggested items to be photographed from unusual perspectives. People learned to *see*—really *see*—downtown. One week later we met for another workshop, where the participants created collages and edit-

ed their proofs for final enlargements. The project enabled people of diverse backgrounds and ages to work as a team, to see through different eyes and views, to explore the unknown aspect of downtown, and to express it all through the eye of the camera.

In addition to the fresh ideas and photos of the participants, Jesse DeMartino and I contributed to the exhibition through the eyes of professional photographers. For over three years, Jesse DeMartino has been documenting the lives of a small group of Houston skateboarders. A skateboarder himself for more than half of his life, DeMartino photographs these youths in their homes, at local skate parks, and—most significantly—in downtown Houston, where the rich concrete landscape serves as a kind of playground for the skateboarders. My desire to work with the community and my passion for photography helped me to really explore downtown to the core. In conclusion, I realized that as this downtown grows through its changes, I also grow and evolve within myself.

Thanks to FotoFest for their support, and to Foley's and the Houston Chronicle for the historical photographs.

Vivian Lee
Curator

Rush, 1997
Vivian Lee
Silver Gelatin Print

Untitled, 1996
Jesse DeMartino
Silver Gelatin Print

GERALD D. HINES COLLEGE OF ARCHITECTURE GALLERY

Saving Salamone
By Edward Shaw and Tomas Shaw

This is the first photographic overview ever to be shown of the bizarre architectural designs of Francisco Salamone (1898-1959), an Argentine civil engineer who worked for the government of the Buenos Aires Province from 1936 to 1940. Salamone, a close friend of Governor Manuel Fresco, covered the Pampa with his three specialties: town halls, slaughter houses and cemetery portals. He is unique in the history of Argentine architecture; no one knows where he got his inspiration. Certainly publications from Europe influenced his vision, forming the essence of his authoritarian blend of Art Deco, embellished with clock towers and avenging angels.

 The purpose of this exhibit goes beyond just reviving the work of this forgotten master. Not only should we remember Salamone as an ambitious designer and builder—over 60 buildings in 25 towns built in four years. There are three steps still to be taken: 1) to restore as much of the work as possible; 2) by making Francisco Salamone known abroad, his local importance grows, to encourage the natives of the towns, where he built, to take a more positive view of his works; and 3) to create the proper infrastructure so

that travelers and tourists can visit the work. These are goals that this exhibition proposes to accomplish in its venue in Argentina. In the United States, the objective is to share this unusual body of work with both architects and art lovers in hopes of generating more interest in other unexpected cultural manifestations from Latin America.

Edward Shaw

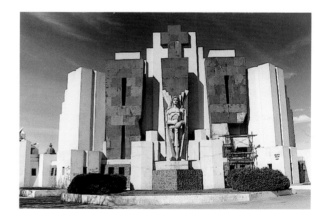

Cemetery Portal, 1996-1997
Edward Shaw and Tomas Shaw
Azul, Province of Buenos Aires, Argentina
Chromogenic Print

Slaughter House, 1996-1997
Edward Shaw and Tomas Shaw
Azul, Province of Buenos Aires, Argentina
Chromogenic Print

City Hall, 1996-1997
Edward Shaw and Tomas Shaw
Guamini, Province of Buenos Aires, Argentina
Chromogenic Print

WORTHAM CENTER

Dark Edges — Kimberly Gremillion

More often than not, theatre photography seems lifeless and posed. These photographs are alive. These photographs look dangerous—yet beautiful. Art photographing art.

Gregory Boyd, artistic director for the Alley Theater

. . . She knows how to capture the art of the moment. Her photographs of the theater cut to the emotional essence of each subject.

David Gockley, general director of the Houston Grand Opera

. . . transforming the performing arts to render a new visual dimension. The results are often haunting, beautiful, surreal, and always powerful.

Toby Mattox, executive director for the Performing Arts

The photographs from *Dark Edges* were inspired by productions from the Alley Theater, the Houston Grand Opera, and the Society for the Performing Arts.

Kimberly Gremillion

Hands #2, 1997
Kimberly Gremillion
Silver Gelatin Print

ORANGE SHOW AND THE INERI FOUNDATION

Four Wheels, One Eye: Art Cars in the Eyes of the Image Makers

THE ART CAR AND THE PHOTOGRAPH

The art car is a factory-made artifact transformed by an artist into a cultural artifact. A photograph of an art car is also a cultural artifact, but with a significant difference. It is a step even further removed from the factory commodity.

The art car is a form of either folk art, sculpture, or assemblage and is a subversive social statement. As art, the form reflects a multiplicity of influences, such as low-riders, racers, Jesus buses and hippie vans, as well as such art styles as surrealism, abstract expressionism, and post-modernism.

The transformation of a factory-made commodity into a personal work of art implies a transfer of power from the corporation to the individual. It is the individual announcing to the powers-that-be that he or she exists as a free individual, not as a consumer or political object.

The photograph of an art car is either a document or a work of art in its own right. As an artist, the photographer goes beyond the image before him or her in order to create a personal statement or metaphor. Otherwise the photograph would be simply a "mug shot" of an existing work of art.

Through creative photography, the aesthetic and social content of the art car becomes an intimate reflection of the photographer's own vision, one that may or may not reflect or extend the vision of the art car artist. Consider, for example, the following: Maurice Roberts' erotic close-up of the door of Mike Robbins' Introvert; Amalia Blyth's humanistic portrait of a low-rider, Eliseo Hilario, Jr., enveloped by his vehicle; Irvin Tepper's intensification of the religious content of Ann Harithas' Mona Lupe; Philip Taplin's psychedelic rendering of Jeff Lockheed's dashboard; Dick Craig's mystical interpretation of Nestor Topchy's art car; and George Hixson's politically charged photograph of the David Koresh Mobile.

All of these photographs are as unique in their own way as is the art that is their subject, and all may be appreciated for themselves as well as for the way they amplify or interpret the image content and context of the cultural artifacts that they portray. Is it not extraordinary that by the simple gesture of taking a photograph, the photographer brings about a deeper visual experience of the art car and at the same time is able to create an intimate and aesthetically independent work of art?

James Harithas

THE ORANGE SHOW AND THE INERI FOUNDATION

At the Orange Show, we are interested in the art car as a kin to monumental handmade environments. They both share characteristics such as the transformation of one's immediate environment with found objects into a personal statement and the stretching of the bounds of acceptable ornamentation. Thirteen years after our first art car program, we are so pleased to present this exhibition of photographs of art cars with the Ineri Foundation. Our early interest was inspired in part by an exhibition mounted by Ineri's founder, Ann Harithas; in part by the art cars themselves that dotted the Houston streets and Texas highways in the early 1980s; and in past by the work of photographers who captured images of remarkable cars that are no longer around. The life span of an automobile is relatively short. The life span of an art car is often even shorter. Photographs, however, have much longer life spans. This exhibition honors the photographers who capture this "movement" and whose images are lasting impressions.

Susanne Theis, Jennifer McKay
The Orange Show

Ripper the Friendly Shark parked at The Orange Show, 1994
Michael Kuchta
Type C Print

God, Guns, and Government: David Koresh Mobile by Mike Scranton, 1993
George Hixson
Silver Gelatin Print

The Introvert, by Mike Robbins, 1989
Maurice Roberts

Zocalo Ziggurat della Azteca by Nester Topchy, 1993
Dick Craig
Color Transparency

Mona Lupe by Ann Harithas, 1995
Irving Tepper
Type C Print

1962 Impala by Eliseo Hilario, Jr., 1995
Amalia Blyth
Type C Print

Hommage to Timothy Leary, 1995
Phillip Taplin
Color Transparency

UNIVERSITY OF ST. THOMAS JONES GALLERY

Chapel of St. Basil, Under Construction:
Artistic Documentary by Valentin L. Gertsman

I documented the construction of Philip Johnson's Jewel-Chapel of St. Basil with my camera. The project has led to this exhibit of forty cibachrome photographs.

Back home in Moscow in the early thirties, inside my little toy box between wooden cubes, metal construction tidbits, and other boyish belongings, was a head of V. Lenin. It was hard as a rock, made of greenish clay and about the same size as a goose egg. My mother told me it was my creation. So my relationship with art goes back beyond my own recollection.

As a child and adolescent, and throughout my medical career, drawing portraits, landscapes, and skylines had always been a part of my life.

I left Moscow for Houston in 1974. One day in 1978, while cleaning the drawers of my desk, I came across three small branches of wood that my eight-year-old daughter Julia and I found in a forest near Moscow in 1973. The longer I looked at those pieces of wood, the more erotic they seemed. So I decided to mount them on some sort of pedestal and apply a special liquid to them for protection. That marked the beginning of my "career" as a "driftwood sculptor."

Two years later I sold my first sculpture. Before giving it to the purchaser, I decided to take a picture of it for my records—but at the time, I didn't even own a camera! So I asked a Russian artist friend of mine to lend me his camera, an old Mamiya.

Looking through the lens of that camera for the first time, I immediately understood that photography was another artistic medium through which I could further develop my creativity. My first photographs were of my own sculptures, and then strange objects found on the beaches, in the forest, in friends' backyards, and even on compost heaps.

One morning in 1981, my American friend invited me to go downtown to take some pictures with him. I agreed, because Houston's architecture and monumental sculptures had always impressed me. For me, Houston has always been the city of the 21st century.

This became the start of my "urban theme" in photography. Some of my photographs simply document architectural concepts, while others—especially the more recent ones—have become pure abstract images. Over time, some of the images have taken on strong symbolic or fantastic meanings of their own, such as Star Wars, Genesis, and others.

I now create an endlessly mysterious and harmonious universe of my own, using my 35mm Minolta RST 201 with a 28mm lens, Kodachrome 64 films, and Superchrome prints.

Valentin Gertsman

GALLERIES

GALLERIES

4

ARCHWAY GALLERY

Alternatives
by Billie Mercer

Ideas germinate like seeds. It takes time. Time for all the elements to fall into place. Several years ago, I became interested in how images in alternative processes evoked a different recognition and understanding of the image. After acquiring a 60-year-old view camera, I began to produce 5x7 negatives to explore the nuances within my work using a process called Argyrotype. While I expected the printed image to have a different feeling, I also found that subjects spoke to me differently. These warm-brown images reveal everyday objects and places with quiet elegance and invite the viewer to explore the forms and shapes and textures. In doing so, the viewer will find the opportunity for a dialogue, or see a humanistic quality in the objects, or open the door on a memory.

Billie Mercer

Diversity from the *Pear* series
Billie Mercer
Argyrotype Print

JOHN CLEARY GALLERY

Paul Caponigro

"To penetrate and record, even if only reflectively through an idea-image, that which takes place in, over, under, around, and through nature, is to feel the intangible, the somewhere in-between, the what is and the what I am, the interaction between visible and invisible. This is what I look for—what I am interested in. I am concerned with what grows out of interaction."

Paul Caponigro

Paul Caponigro is clearly one of the contemporary masters of photography, creating some of the finest prints in the medium. They awaken us to the beauty of objects and to the moods of a landscape, and they

Scots Thistle, 1958
Paul Caponigro
Silver Gelatin Print

sensitize our vision to the subtleties of light. Caponigro's images evoke the invisible sources behind physical phenomena, the reality we cannot see penetrating the one we do. Before his camera lens, nature unmasks her sense of conscious awareness and quiet purpose. Silence responds with energy and rhythms from beyond which nature shapes her movements. It is his artistic passion to have us set aside our daily habits of mind, to engage our intuition and apprehend a wider reality, a reality both veiled and yet revealed by our physical surroundings.

Caponigro's images reflect a metaphysical sensibility— an apple glimmering like the sky at night, a stream that recalls a curtain of appearances, a stone megalith that suggests levitation and spiritual flight. He also captures the transcendent quietude of billowing clouds over idyllic pastoral settings and the classical topography of France, Ireland, and Italy. Caponigro perceives a beauty not only pleasing to the eye, but also nourishing to the spirit.

As humanity ages, illusions about the world fade and wonder is withdrawn. With rare subtlety, Caponigro's work restores wonder within us. His photographs return us to our senses and affirm our existence in a higher realm.

Sarah Irwin

From our Celebrating Color exhibition, the gallery is also presenting Jeffrey Becom, with previously unseen and favorite images.

ARTABLES GALLERY

In the Public Eye
by Dave Wilson

Artables Gallery presents this series of photographs exploring the nature of public art in Houston, Texas. The subject matter is taken from outdoor murals, sculpture, and spaces altered by local artists. I think of these photos as documents, making note of the art that plays a part in our daily lives. Some of these compositions are no longer in existence, having been painted over, removed, vandalized, or deteriorated—as will be the case for all of them in due time. They are who we are, representing our culture and our time.

Dave Wilson

Rita, Futon Girl
1665 Westheimer at Dunlavy,
Dave Wilson
Composition by Kevin Bapp, Commissioned by Debora Smail

ARTHUR MEYERSON PHOTOGRAPHY

"True Grit" Photographs of Working Cowboys
by Arthur Meyerson

Beginning in 1988, I was fortunate enough to begin documenting that "most American" of American icons, the cowboy. It was, in many ways, the fulfillment of a childhood dream. Hollywood movies and advertising campaigns have also helped keep this dream alive. But it was while photographing the annual spring and fall round-ups that I truly felt that I was living in a Charles Russell painting, as most of that process has not changed in over a hundred years. Honesty, integrity, and wit marked the character of all the men photographed.

But the unfortunate reality is that this unique lifestyle is disappearing. Long days, hard work, loss of knowledge of the land and livestock, and low pay have combined to create a shortage of these rugged individuals.

As this era rides off into the sunset, let these photographs stand as a testament to the true grit of these men who lived the dream.

Arthur Meyerson

Cowboys Branding, 1997
Arthur Meyerson
Color Transparency

MD MODERN GALLERY

Recent Work
by Bob Wade

I collect vintage black-and-white photo postcards of Tex-Mex, rodeo, or simply "unusual" subjects. After cropping and scaling these images according to my sensibilities, I enlarge them onto photosensitized fabric.

Once the fabric has been stretched, I utilize my academic training as a painter by airbrushing transparent layers of acrylic color over the surface images, thus "bringing them to new life" with respect and affection for the original photo.

By employing muted tones reminiscent of pre-technicolor movie films, I can achieve a remarkable number of visual effects with these large-scale photoworks. Humor and irony also pervade the work.

Bob Wade

Bonny Blackpool Bathers, 1997
Bob Wade
Acrylic on Photo Linen

The Mind's Eye
by Fannie Tapper

With a lifelong interest in poetic narrative, my por-
traits-tableaux focus on the human condition and the
discovery of the self. My work is concerned with the
evolution of the sentient being from innocent childhood to pensive youth to disenchanted old age. It mirrors the rise, flowering, and decline of sexuality; relationships and gender roles; illness, loss, and longing.
All the while, it extols the indomitable human spirit.
My images, regardless of subject, bespeak human presence or absence.

My scenes are fragmented fictions, open-ended docu-
dramas, elliptical dialogues, provoking visual and
intellectual elaboration. Like myths and fairytales, the
images are more suggestive than descriptive, more
evocative than factual.

Fannie Tapper

Bean-Vine Girl (From *a Day in Portland*), 1997
Fannie Tapper
Silver Gelatin Print

McMURTREY GALLERY

Bridge of Sighs
Images by Keith Carter

Keith Carter . . . defines his concerns as those of the poet, and uses the medium of photography to address those concerns. As such, though he may eventually manifest epic tendencies, he now functions as a lyric poet, a dowsing rod for that "imagination in the boondocks" of which he spoke and a wellspring of it himself. Patiently generating a quiet poetry of solitude and survival, he reveals to us that ritual, magic, and invention live everywhere that people call home, and that, simultaneously, we remain not that different from what we once were, ever inclined to jump into the mud and piss naked in the swamp, still one form of animal among others.

A. D. Coleman, October 1996

Raven, 1996
Keith Carter
Toned Silver Gelatin Print

ANYA TISH GALLERY

"Collection II"
Grzegorz Banaszkiewicz

The old courtyard fountainheads are favorite motifs in my work. Almost every courtyard in the city I grew up in had one of them. For the neighborhood children, the fountains were the best places to play. For the thousands of pilgrims coming to pray to the Black Madonna of Jasna Gora, they served as a respite.

In the past, the fountainheads were treated with a reverence; placed in stone niches, adorned in rod-iron "dresses," and decorated in architectural details. For years I have been watching them dry up and crumble, their decay aided by passing time and human indifference. Visiting these sites is like visiting good old friends. I "portray" my fountains with a deserving objectiveness and a documentary detail; however, they evade the objectiveness and still live their quiet lives filled with secrets, moods, and dramatic events.

Grzegorz Banaszkiewicz

Collection II, 1996
Grzegorz Banaszkiewicz
Silver Gelatin Print

Discovering Third Ward,
Yates Magnet School Photography Exhibition

The selection of works for this exhibition was drawn from several hundred photographs taken by high school students working with Ray Carrington, the instructor of photography who launched the project of photographing Houston's historical African-American neighborhood in 1993. The resulting body of work has already given the material for three exhibitions presented by the Museum of Fine Arts, Houston and titled *Eye on Third Ward* (July 1995, September 1996, September 1997). Portraits of old people, children, and pets, as well as images of favorite places of play, places of worship, and ordinary street corners, provide the viewer with an intimate insight into the everyday life of a unique neighborhood. The process of discovery takes place on several levels. By discovering the spirit of their neighborhood through the camera lens, the students discover their own abilities to observe and record. The viewer is given an opportunity to discover as well. Not only is one transported to the very life of a community, but one also is witness to the photographer's transformation.

Anya Tish

Untitled, 1997
Angela Williams
Silver Gelatin Print

NEW GALLERY

Desires and Fears
Images by David Levinthal

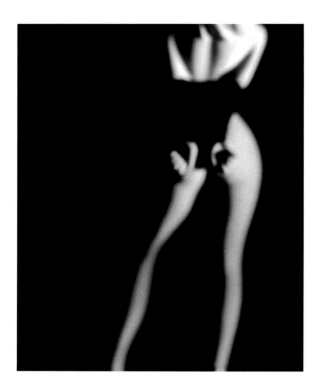

Desire, 1990-1991
David Levinthal
Type C Print

Utilizing toy models for his subject matter, David Levinthal reflects basic truths about the human condition while creating a parallel fantasy world of soft-focus dream nostalgia and lurid nightmare. In some of his work, such as the *American Beauties* and *The Wild West*, an idealized Americana is presented as a "Saturday morning" view of American archetypes simplified and monumentalized through a basic plastic form. In works from his *Desire* series, the models are more obscured, conjuring up images that seem to spring from a subconscious realm of lusts and passions. On the harsh realistic theme of the *Mein Kampf* photographs, the images are chillingly powerful in their use of shadow silhouette and narrow focus to heighten the dream-state reality of a holocaust that still seems unimaginable. This current exhibition at New Gallery by David Levinthal will feature works from various series that have most recently been exhibited in his retrospective at the International Center of Photography in New York.

Thom Andriola

PARKERSON GALLERY

Shadow Play
Images by Kimberly Gremillion

Light seeps through the dark curtain giving only a hint as to what will emerge. Poised in the realm between darkness and light, my images reveal an unseen world. By transforming the event into black-and-white, the drama of the moment is enhanced.

These images are metaphors for human feelings and actions. The clown is every man. Behind his smile lies sadness. The couple embracing foreshadows conflict, while the tightrope walker traverses a frail line in search of equilibrium.

There are many archetypes hidden within the dark edges: the hoop of fire, the shadow of the spotlight, the solitary figure gazing through a veiled portal. Shadows convey aspects of the indiscernible, evoking an emotional response in the viewer. These fleeting images shift from positive to negative space creating rhythm and tension.

Memories from childhood resonate in my work. My photographs draw my dreams.

Kimberly Gremillion

Shadow #2, 1997
Kimberly Gremillion
Silver Gelatin Print

EVIN THAYER STUDIOS

AIDS Foundation Houston Photo Project
Evin Thayer

As a third-generation Houstonian, I believe that Houston's greatest asset is its people. Whether politician, humanitarian, entrepreneur, medical or science pioneer, philanthropist, sports personality, or entertainer, I am dedicated to recognizing these people and their contributions, thus developing *The Evin Thayer Celebrity Series*. This is a work-in-progress celebrating outstanding native and adopted Houstonians who have achieved success in their field of work. Technical expertise, a sensitive eye, and high standard of artistic quality have enabled me to capture the spirit of those photographed.

As with the *Celebrity Series*, I am dedicated to making a difference in the community. My staff and I work to create fund-raising events benefiting worthy organizations such as the AIDS Foundation, Casa de Esperanza, the Bering Community Service Foundation, the Assistance Fund, the Houston Symphony, Diffa, the Animal Fund, and many others. My photographs have appeared in publications such as *Houston Metropolitan*, *Texas Monthly*, *DBA*, *Houston Health and Fitness*, *L'Entrée*, *Texas Woman*, *Inside Houston*, and the Media Ink Publications. My work has been featured in the *Professional Photographers of America* magazine and I have been a guest lecturer on fashion photography at *FotoFest 96*. Regardless of the format, I strive to stay on the "cutting edge."

Evin Thayer

Sharon K. Wagner, 1996
AIDS Foundation Houston Photo Essay
Evin Thayer
Silver Gelatin Print

GREMILLION & CO. FINE ART, INC.

Exploding Into Light
by Amanda Means

Flower Number 33, 1995
Amanda Means
Photogram

Memory of Loss

I grew up on a farm, close to nature, observing the changes of seasons and weather and the shifting light on the fields and in the woods.

I move to New York City to study art.

We lose our family farm.

My father dies.

My move to a highly urban environment intensified my sense of loss. My photographs of vegetation—plant forms and flowers—are a metaphor for this feeling of bereavement.

Amanda Means

Recent Work by Debbie Fleming Caffery

The central element in my photography has been the attempt to
visually articulate the ineffable.
My images often involve people
and landscapes partially obscured
by fog, smoke, or fire, and are
long exposures frequently
blurred in order to emphasize
the mood. Certain weather conditions, balances of light and
shadow, and the singularity of my
subjects resonate with me and
thus form the springboard for
the creation of a complete photograph.

I try to instill into my photographs a visual sense of what is
beautiful, heart wrenching, and
confusing—an emotional organization of feelings, texture, and
light.

Debbie Fleming Caffery

Roberto, 1994
Debbie Flemming Caffery
Silver Gelatin Print

THOMAS V. ROBINSON/
ROBINSON GALLERIES

Abroad
by Terry Vine

Moody, ethereal, and impressionistic, Terry Vine's black-and-white photographs of European scenes are evocative of images shot in the 1920s and 1930s. More than a reflection of what Europe is like today, they are a rediscovery of where its soul lives. In the very shadowy nature of these photographs, the viewer finds traces of the past, details of things much loved and often overlooked in the hustle and bustle.

In harkening back to an earlier time and an earlier photographic style, Terry Vine also has given expression to his own photographic "voice." Much to his amazement, photographs that he had tucked away in boxes thinking that they had no commercial value are finding an appreciative audience among corporate and advertising clients.

A commercial photographer in Houston for more than a decade, Vine had developed a successful career shooting for corporate annual reports, brochures, and advertising. As with many photographers, he kept separate those projects he undertook for personal satisfaction and those that he did on assignment. "I thought it was interesting personal work, but I never showed it to any clients." At first, he let only a few close friends and clients see them. "I remember talking to my rep then, saying, "We'll never show this to anyone, but I sure love this work." And she said, "I'm going to show it."

What happened next caught Vine by surprise. "Clients said they wanted to see some more personal things: 'We want you to shoot this building like you did the streets of Paris,' they'd say." Gradually, his personal projects found their way into his work portfolio.

Vine's trips to Europe have taken on new interest now that his travel photos have been discovered. When there, he likes to shoot in black and white, preferably in adverse weather. "I see Europe in black and white in my mind's eye because it is so old and there is so much stone and texture," he says. When it is cloudy and dreary out, I can shoot all day. The textures and tones I am looking for show up better when the lighting is soft." Even when a photo was taken in bright sunlight, Vine will manipulate the image in the darkroom. "I shot the trees in Tuscany in the middle of the day. Originally, we printed it high contrast, but then went back into the darkroom and printed it darker, lowered the contrast, and flattened it so it would look like it was shot in the middle of the night."

With a show coming up and more clients telling Vine they want him to bring his personal vision to the assignment, Vine is finding that he is becoming known for a style distinctively his own. Interestingly, it wasn't something he had to go out and invent; it was in him all along.

Delphine Hirasuna,
NEO Magazine, *June 1997*

Statue, Place de la Concorde, 1996
Terry Vine
Sepia-toned Silver Gelatin Print

SICARDI-SANDERS GALLERY

Traces on the Glass: The Photography of Geraldo de Barros

In his 1925 essay *The Dehumanization of Art*, José Ortega y Gasset, one of the first theoreticians of the avant-garde, drew an analogy between the new art and a translucent glass which became increasingly dehumanized as it became opaque. According to Ortega, the new art prevented us from viewing the world behind the glass and forced us to reflect instead upon the "vitreous" medium itself. This process described by Ortega had an ambivalent effect on Latin American avant-garde artists because some interpreted the totally opaque and dehumanized work of art (pure art) as a desirable goal, while others saw it as a hurdle to be avoided if art was to share in the human experience. It is hard today to gauge the enormous impact of Ortega's ideas, which were widely discussed in Latin America as late as the 1960s.

In the late 1940s and early 1950s, Geraldo de Barros (b. Brazil, 1923), a consummate Brazilian modern painter, taught himself a way of using the photographic negative as a technique for printmaking—on a par with woodcut, etching, and lithography. Yet his print matrix, the negative, received the imprint both from the lens and from his own interventions. In a move that today may be regarded by some as postmodern, de Barros disengaged the photographic image from its purely referential function, manipulating the negative in order to footnote the act of photographic representation. De Barros blended the artificial sketch with the visual datum and, by so doing, he was proposing a way out of the misleading dichotomy that effectively split Latin American artists between those advocating art-for-art's-sake and those defending humanistic art. With very few exceptions—Geraldo de Barros being one of them—in Latin American photography this polarized way of thinking prevailed until the late 1980s.

De Barros' groundbreaking photographic work was ignored for decades, until his daughter, Fabiana de Barros, became instrumental in organizing a retrospective for him at the Musée de l'Elysée of Lausanne. With this exhibition at Sicardi-Sanders, the work of this visionary Brazilian artist will be seen in the United States for the very first time.

Fernando Castro, Curator

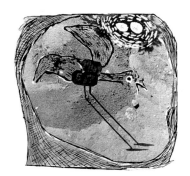

Untitled, 5/15, 1949
Tatuapé Cemetery, São Paulo, Brazil
Geraldo de Barros
Drawing on a Negative with Drypoint & China Ink
Printed 1997

Tribute to Stravinski, 4/15, 1949
Itu, São Paulo, Brazil
Geraldo de Barros
Drawing on a Negative with Drypoint & China Ink
Printed 1997

Untitled, 3/15, 1951
Paris, France
Geraldo de Barros
Silver Gelatin Print
Printed 1997

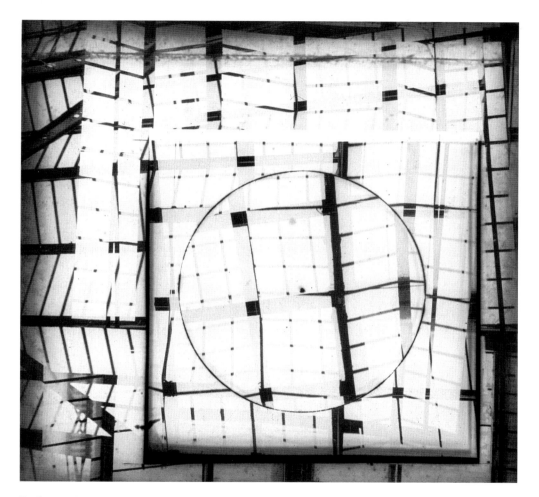

Fotoforma, 4/15, 1950
Estacão d Luz, São Paulo, Brazil
Geraldo de Barros
Copy from Cut Negative, Pressed between Two Glass Plates
Printed 1995

MOODY GALLERY

The Trouble with Arcadia
By Suzanne Bloom and Ed Hill (MANUAL)

*But when, at Zephyrs' call, joyous Summer sends both sheep and goats
to the glades and pastures, let us haste to the cool fields, as the morn-
ing-star begins to rise, while the day is young, while the grass is hoar,
and the dew on the tender blade most sweet to the cattle.*

Virgil, Georgics Book III

In our current extended project we are trying to
loosen the concept (and reality) of "Arcadia" from its
unexamined niche in world history. While Virgil's
shepherds roamed in classical pastoral settings,
Technology had already visited the fields and woods
where they watched over their sheep, goats, or cattle.
And by the time Nicolas Poussin painted his various
scenes of Arcadian shepherds in the 17th century, rural
industry had modified the landscape even more extensively. Arcadia evolved as the construction of a privi-
leged class of urbanites who longed for a simpler life
in a primordial place. All they could do was recreate
its appearance as they fancied—or wished—it had been.

The concept lingers into our age of highly advanced
computational technology. It is from the deliberate
perspective and using the protean tools of electronic
culture that we are attempting to revisualize and
reconstruct ancient Arcady.

MANUAL

Blue Shepherd, 1997
Suzanne Bloom and Ed Hill (MANUAL)
Type C Print

ROBERT McCLAIN & CO

Sexual Desire
Images by Nobuyoshi Araki

INDEPENDENT EXHIBIT

This exhibition of Nobuyoshi Araki's most recent portfolio of images, titled *Sexual Desire*, is based on a body of work installed at the Museum Für Moderne Kust Frankfurt am Main in Frankfurt, Germany in June 1996.

Araki continues to explore dual themes of a confined, confused urban Tokyo and images of Japanese women, staged and posed in states of bondage and explicit sexuality.

Araki attempts to relate the repression of Japanese life, it's crushing urban mass, and the exquisite deprivation and control exacted on Japanese women.

Robert McClain

Sexual Desire, 1996
Nobuyoshi Araki
Iris Color Print, 27/30

Images by Claudette Champbrun Goux, Will Michels, Roger Stone

This series, entitled *Impressions/Reflections*, is a play on the mirror effect of the water, capturing natural forms and visual impressions. The photographs were taken in Brazos Bend State Park, between Houston and Austin, Texas. They were shot often on the same day but at different times and under changing skies and lighting.

Monet observed and painted the play of light on haystacks and the color variations of the waterlilies at Giverny. The great photographer Atget returned to Ville-D'Avray in the footsteps of another painter to photograph "Corot's ponds". This work is an homage and an additional footnote to a process begun by the impressionists and carried on by photography.

Claudette Champbrun Goux

These portraits are the result of a spontaneous, ongoing project and stem from early insecurities with having my picture taken. They reflect me within the privacy of my home, resulting in quiet, introspective, and sometimes disturbing images. Some document mundane activities such as bathing and shaving. All depict a struggle I have with my own image and how other people perceive it. They depict a struggle with who I am and where I am going, trying to find an identity lost somewhere in the past.

I use my apartment, bedroom, and bathroom as studios. I do not look through the camera. These images are not "composed". Rolls of film are taken spontaneously and quickly. Some, routinely every Friday upon wakening, others randomly, as if to try and capture something off guard. These photographs are views into my life and home.

Will Michels

My love for the medium of photography as well as the actual process of shooting and printing manifests itself in my romantically surreal, almost impressionistic style of image making. In my work, I create a visual vignette, a daydream, and an optical oasis. When I'm successful, the viewer's consciousness is transposed to a different reality, a timeless place of peace and beauty.

I have been shooting black-and-white infrared film since 1985, and I appreciate the qualities of depth and texture this film gives my subjects, as well as a dreamlike quality with its soft highlights and large grain. The prints are printed on a warm-toned paper that is then split-toned. This process reinforces a surreal quality which further distances the viewer from reality. The actual content of the image is secondary to the mood created by the process. The statement of the work is inherent in the use of light, form, and texture.

Roger Stone

STEPHEN L. CLARK GALLERY AT JOAN WICH & CO. GALLERY

The Edge of Time: Fotografías de México / Photographs of Mexico by Mariana Yampolsky

Mariana Yampolsky's work is essential to her life. When she opened the window on her very first morning in Mexico City and saw a bougainvillea blossoming against the white wall outside, she decided "this is my country." And when she walked through the bustle and energy of the downtown streets—Cuauhtemotzin, Donceles, San Juan de Letrán—among the lottery ticket vendors, the street peddlers, the deliverymen shouting "Careful there! Give me room!," she chose her people without a second thought.

Yampolsky's relation to those she photographs is direct and vital: to the woman who looks at her while shelling corn, to the bride in the short skirt and white ankle socks, to the four old women waiting for the priest. They come right through the camera and say to our face, "Look! Here I am and there you are. And what are you going to do about it? What are you going to do about my wrinkled hands, my ragged shawl, my eyes like embers? How will you go on living as before?"

Elena Poniatowska
Excerpt from *Roots and Pathways*

Esperando al padre, 1987
(Waiting for the Priest)
Mariana Yampolsky
Silver Gelatin Print

Images from the Making of Lonesome Dove, the Miniseries: The Photographs of Bill Wittliff

Bill Wittliff is, quite simply, a man of vision. Vision that pulls words off pages and materializes them on a television or movie screen. Vision that makes still images, captured in a small camera, transcend our modern reality and take us back one hundred years.

Wittliff's photographs from the making of *Lonesome Dove* are pieces out of time. The painterly qualities of these sepia-toned prints belie the modern materials with which they are made. Wittliff prints each image with its own character: heroic portraits with open sky, haunting landscapes at first light, horses driven through water and dust. The atmosphere is rich and the characters—Gus, Call, Pea Eye, Lorena, Clara, and all the others as well—are alive with such familiarity that we think we know them, which we do.

Stephen L. Clark

Front Porch, 1988
Bill Wittliff
Silver Gelatin Print

HARRIS GALLERY

Gary Faye—Color Photographs

After twenty years of exhibiting black-and-white photographs, Gary Faye will introduce his color work at Harris Gallery during FotoFest 1998. While Faye has not exhibited color previously, he has shot color throughout his career. Some of the early subjects parallel his black-and-white work in the dunes series, western canyons, and other subjects from the American landscape. The most recent color work hails primarily from northern Italy and southern France.

In Italy, Faye views the architecture of Burano—brightly colored, heavily textured, accentuated by the raking light—as the palette for his work. He succeeds in capturing the pulse of this small island village while also elevating the images to studies in abstraction and geometry. In France, the soft colors and sweeping fields contrast with the village architecture and its subdued tones and ancient references. Both countries provide an ideal balance of ancient architecture, historical villages, and vibrant culture which Faye manages to capture through his lens.

Faye's color photographs, like his black-and-white work, are distinguished by the dramatic use of light defining both the rural landscape and the urban environment. However, this work boasts a magical play of surface, light, and color that gives these photographs almost a painterly quality. His compositions are sensitive to both texture and form, with strong angular shapes juxtaposed to soft tactile textures.

Gary Faye shoots his work in a variety of formats, including 35mm, 4 x 5, and large panoramas. The print type is cibachrome, which Faye favors because it accentuates the contrast and color saturation of the photographs.

Harrison Itz

"I have always loved the intensity of black and white, the immediate abstraction and drama, the focus on light and mood. I thought it distilled things to a sort of concentrate—a double espresso of life. Although most of my influences over the past twenty years have been black and white, I sometimes found myself reaching for color to express something I couldn't touch any other way. I didn't reflect on it much — just did it. Later, while painting on some Polaroid transfers, I thought more about it and realized I was after an emotion— a colored feeling. Yes, it would work in black and white, but the color statement would be different. It conjured up other feelings. This show is a collection of some of those moments."

Gary Faye

Clothesline, Burano, Italy, 1997
Gary Faye

3 Boats, Burano, Italy, 1997
Gary Faye
Cibachrome Print

INMAN GALLERY

Recent Work: Jane Hinton

Jane Hinton alters our perception of industrial structures—mainly bridges—through the use of multiple
frames from a stereo camera to produce a single
image. At times, the structure of the bridge can disappear into the black edges of the multi-frame murals,
adding to the sense of a single shot. With closer
inspection, physically impossible bridge structures are
revealed to be artist-structured images. By varying
points of view, Hinton composes soaring, dizzying,
disorienting images that cause the viewer to take a second look at intrusive industrial hulks. The mechanical
necessity of a bridge's design—its line, weight, and
material—is coaxed into a more lyrical presence. The
bridges that Hinton "builds" guide the viewer's eyes
just as a bridge guides travel. The horizontal expanse
of a bridge is echoed in Hinton's two-and three-frame
horizontal compositions. In *Sun Times Lift Bridge*, the ver-
tical format emphasizes a sense of vertigo through two
very different points of view.

Patrick Reynolds

Sun Times Lift Bridge, 1996
Jane Hinton
Silver Gelatin Print, edition of ten

JAMES GALLERY

Fragmentary Evolutions
Images by Dornith Doherty

Dornith Doherty's recent body of work is the result of her drive to retain the mystery and complexity of life through the medium of photography. The images she creates are stunningly beautiful and visually intriguing. They make us pause, and we cannot but ask ourselves "What are we looking at and why are these works so compelling?"

Many of them visually echo sonograms, Indonesian puppet shadow dances, Dutch still-life paintings, and nineteenth-century European fabric designs. This mixture of scientific peering and artistic portrayal is no accident. In fact, Doherty is self-consciously paying attention to the ways art and science explore the world and, from this research, she merges her study of both onto the same plane: the photograph.

We can all remember the first time we looked through a microscope: adjusting the light, preparing the slide, clipping it in place, getting used to looking down with one eye, and then working the focus. We observed something down there, but we were not quite sure if we had it right. Patterns emerged, things wiggled, and we had never seen anything like it before. As the teacher explained more to us, our wonder expanded and a whole new world of seeing, of possibilities for seeing, emerged. In proportion to our wonder came the knowledge necessary to interpret what we were seeing. Classification became part of our learning as an essential tool for compartmentalizing, much the way scheduling became necessary for ordering daily living.

Systems of ordering are external to our experiences of life in a body. Nature has its own rhythms and patterns, cycles and systems, which Doherty respects and shows. Our classifications coexisting in relation to the natural world can create harmony only when there is fluidity between the two—an ebb and flow between art and science. Someone recently spoke of art and science as entering the same zoo but by different doorways. In Doherty's work, we get to see art and science's zoo from both points of view at the same time.

By unabashedly constructing her images, Doherty states that all constructs are artificial, if not arbitrary. Yet there is nothing arbitrary about the combinations she collates. Through the simultaneous presentation of nature and systems of classification, her photographs have the strange power to evoke our own primordial emotional responses to pain, death, decay, new life, sadness, and celebration. The mystery we all know life to be can never be located succinctly: it lies neither in science nor in art, but . . . it lies behind them both and in the chaos and order of daily living. In these photographs, we need not be artificially linear; we can be ourselves and honestly face our realities. We can know that the beauty of Doherty's photographs is present, even if hidden for a little while.

Joanna Weber
Assistant Curator
European and Contemporary Art
Yale University Art Gallery

Untitled, 1997
Dornith Doherty
Chromogenic Color Print

BARBARA DAVIS GALLERY AT PENNZOIL PLACE

Contemporary Brazilian Photography from The Joaquim Paiva Collection

ARTISTS: GERALDO DE BARROS, SANDRA BORDIN, ROCHELLE COSTI, JEAN GUIMARÃES, CLAUDIA JAGUARIBE, RUTH LIFSCHITS, LUCIA MINDLIN LOEB, RUBENS MANO, JOSE MEDEIROS, MARIO CRAVO NETO, KENJI OTA, ROGELIO REIS, ROSÂNGELA RENNÓ, SEBASTIÃO SALGADO AND CASSIO VASCONCELLOS

Forty-eight works by 15 Brazilian photographers are featured in this exhibition of The Joaquim Paiva Collection. This exhibition includes work by these mid-career and established photographers: Geraldo de Barros, Sandra Bordin, Rochelle Costi, Jean Guimarães, Claudia Jaguaribe, Ruth Lifschits, Lucia Mindlin Loeb, Rubens Mano, Jose Medeiros, Mario Cravo Neto, Kenji Ota, Rogelio Reis, Rosângela Rennó, Sebastião Salgado, and Cassio Vasconcellos

Joaquim Paiva, a photographer himself, started acquiring photography in 1978. Since then, he has assembled a notable collection of 1,650 images by 130 Brazilian photographers. The collection spans the past 30 years with an emphasis on the 1980s and 1990s. The work ranges from art to documentary photography, from self-expression to cultural reflection and includes both traditional and experimental approaches. The diversity and innovation of the work reflects the vitality of the contemporary photographic practice in Brazil.

Joaquim Paiva grew up in Rio de Janeiro. He is a diplomat for the Brazilian government and has traveled extensively. Living abroad has given him the opportunity to appreciate his country from a distance and better understand its cultural richness and plurality. Paiva's bibliography includes *Olhares refletidos - diálogo com 25 fotógrafos brasileiros* (1989) and *Aos pés de Batman - poemas* (1994). He received the Acquisition Prize at the VIII National Visual Arts Exhibition in Rio de Janeiro in 1985.

Pampa Risso-Patrón

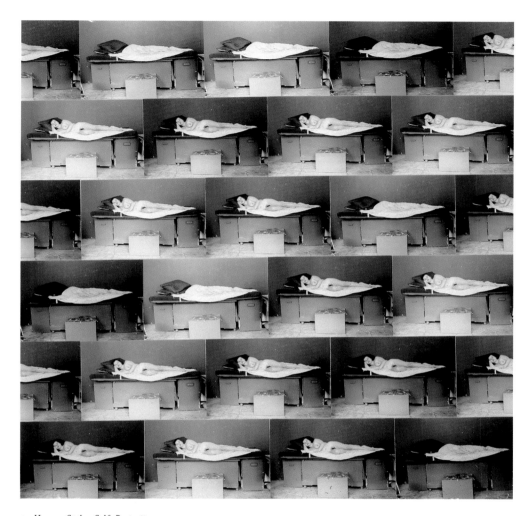

50 Hours: Stolen Self–Portrait, 1992
Rochelle Costi
Chromogenic Print

Tribute to Paul Klee, 1949
Geraldo de Barros
Silver Gelatin Print

Monte Santo, Brasil, 1981
Sebastião Salgado
Silver Gelatin Print

Sea Landscapes, 1993
Cassio Vasconcellos
Silver Gelatin Print

Illuminated Woman, 1988
Rosângela Rennó
Silver Gelatin Print

Mulheres iluminadas

Sacrifice IV, 1989
Mario Cravo Neto
Silver Gelatin Print

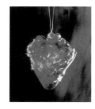

Slaughter: Insistent Dream, 1995
Sandra Bordin
Cibachrome Print

LAWING GALLERY

Field: Images by Uta Barth

Field #20, 1997
Uta Barth
Acrylic Lacquer on Canvas

Field #20 and *Field #21* were originally produced in 1997 for a commissioned "Wall Project" at the Museum of Contemporary Art in Chicago. These two large photographs are the first works of the *Field* series in which the scale of each image begins to approximate that of a film screen. Depicting blurred cityscapes, they have the visual and compositional vocabulary of filmmaking in which the recorded information, freely bleeds off the

Field #21, 1997
Uta Barth
Acrylic Lacquer on Canvas

edge. Both the camera and the (imagined) subject are dynamic, as motion if implied in the unoccupied foreground. As the viewer, one walks into these atmospheric scenes, locations, or backgrounds and stands in the space of action. The work draws attention not only to what is depicted, but also to our own sense of perception and the activity of seeing that which may lie at the periphery of our field of vision.

Sheryl Conkelton

WEEKEND GALLERY

Allusions: Images by John Herrin, Claire Chauvin

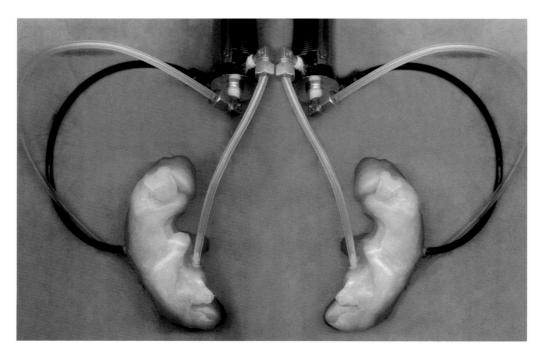

Rorschach Antibiosis, 1997
Claire Chauvin
Digital Print

I strive to explore the world and discover interesting subjects to photograph. Then I coax the image into sharing its magic with the viewer. However, for a work of art to be compelling, it must be easily accessible while remaining a mystery on a deeper level. The best works can never be completely comprehended; that's what keeps them interesting. Photography, or any other medium, is a valid means of expression so long as the medium itself contributes to the validity and meaning of a particular work in a way no other creative endeavor can.

John Herrin

Houston #45, 1995
John Herrin
Type C Print

CORPORATE AND COMMERCIAL SPACES

MOBILE EXHIBIT

CORPORATE &
COMMERCIAL
SPACES

5

Vietnam: Two Views
The Photography of Sandra and Steven Rudy

INDEPENDENT EXHIBIT

On the 1st of April, 1995, my wife, Sandra, and I arrived at Ton So Nhut Airport in Ho Chi Minh City to begin a long-awaited adventure. I had been to Vietnam before. In 1968-69, I was stationed outside of Da Nang, working in the Navy's Pacification program.

During the war, I lived in Tam Toa, a squalid village of lean-to shanties that was home to about 2,500 montagnard families — all war refugees. I was a member of a team of four that provided medical services, dug wells, built schools, and lent a hand in any task or project necessary to meet the refugees' basic needs for survival. From time to time, I also did combat-related photography in I Corps between Da Nang and the DMZ.

For many years, I had wanted to return—not necessarily to photograph Vietnam, but more importantly, to revisit old memories—memories that differed from those of other Americans who shared the Vietnam experience with me. I needed to find out whether my memories had been filtered through rose-colored glasses or if I had simply been fortunate enough to see another side of Vietnam.

The photographs, made in April 1995, and then on a return trip in November 1996, are not an attempt to recreate "the war" as most Americans visualize it, but are simply an attempt to show Americans Vietnam as I see it today—a beautiful country inhabited by attractive, friendly, proud, and hard-working people—not really so different from the Vietnam I experienced in 1968-69.

Steven Jay Rudy

Steven was the first man I met who would talk about his experience in Vietnam. When we met in 1973, I was fascinated by his stories of the war, the country, and the people. I had spent the summers of 1969 through 1971 working in villages in Central America with Amigos de las Américas, a Houston-based organization that sends volunteers to live in villages in Latin America to give immunizations, teach English and good health practices, and dig latrines.

When we decided to make the journey to Vietnam, I was determined to see the country with as an unprejudiced and fresh eye as was possible. I did very little research. I read no histories of the country or the war. This is not my usual approach.

The result was an immediate immersion in a completely new, different, and astoundingly stimulating culture. Had I done my usual research, I might not have noticed the amazing sense of design that the people use in their everyday lives, the way traffic moves like a river along the roads and the streets, the lack of distinctive odors, and the ubiquitous shade of green in the countryside.

The journey was a return for Steven. I saw Vietnam in a completely fresh light with no preconceived ideas. We both see Vietnam as one of the most beautiful countries in the world, with a people who are energetic, warm, and welcoming. This is the Vietnam we have tried to capture in our images.

Sandra R. Rudy

Cham Child, Mekong Delta, 1995
Stephen Jay Rudy
Type 35 Reversal Color Print

Street Scene, Saigon, 1995
Sandra R. Rudy
Silver Gelatin Print

PALACE CAFE AND HOGG GRILL

Portraits and Fashion, The Archives of Milton H. Greene

INDEPENDENT EXHIBIT

During the 1950s and 60s, Milton H. Greene's photographs of high fashion and portraits of celebrities, film stars, artists, and well-known dance and theater personalities were published in most major U.S. publications, including *Vogue*, *Harpers Bazaar*, *Life*, *Look*, *Town & Country*, and *McCalls*. Early in his career, at the age of twenty-three, Greene was called "color photography's wonder boy." He is credited with being one of the photographers who brought fashion photography into the realm of a fine art.

For over a decade, Greene's photography was stored in a vault and remained unavailable to the public. The Archives of Milton H. Greene has begun an extensive restoration process of his work to make it available for exhibition, publication, and collection.

The range of Greene's subjects includes Marilyn Monroe, Marlene Dietrich, Grace Kelly, Sammy Davis, Jr., Sophia Loren, Elizabeth Taylor, Cary Grant, Federico Fellini, Ava Gardner, Queen Elizabeth, Maria Tallchief, Alberto Giacometti, Audrey Hepburn, John F. Kennedy, Laurence Olivier, Paul Newman, and Andy Warhol, among others.

Greene is particularly known for his close friendship, business relationship, and photography of Marilyn Monroe. He first encountered Monroe on assignment for *Look* magazine. They became close friends and in 1953 formed their own film production company, which produced *Bus Stop* and *The Prince and The Showgirl*. Before marrying Arthur Miller, Monroe lived with Greene and his family in Connecticut. During their ten-year working relationship, Greene photographed Monroe in over fifty sessions, including the famous "into the night" sittings. Monroe entrusted Greene with her autobiography called *My Story*. Greene also collaborated with Norman Mailer on a fictional autobiography of Monroe titled *Of Women and Their Elegance*.

Among the 300,000 images in Greene's archive, some are being digitally restored and reproduced in a special collection of Iris inkjet prints.

Joshua Greene
President
The Archive of Milton H. Greene

This exhibition has been produced with the assistance of the Milton H. Greene Archive—Joshua Greene and Sophie Cage; the Palace Cafe/Hogg Grill—Cinda Ward; and FotoFest, Inc.

Marlene Dietrich, Legs, Life Magazine, 1952
Milton H. Greene
Silver Gelatin Print

SOLERO

Friends of FotoFest

Portrait after Leonard #1, 1983-1989
Pavel Banka
Hand-painted Silver Gelatin Print

MARKET SQUARE BAR AND GRILL

Delusional Architecture, Photography by Tracy Hart

I have been photographing the cultural landscape for almost twenty years. My work has focused on the relationship of art and the technology related to music and architecture. This is a juxtaposition that has been historically explored within the art and technology of photography itself. Ansel Adams was trained as a classical pianist, Kodachrome was invented by two musicians, and Edward Weston said: "Whenever I can feel a Bach fugue in my work, I know I have arrived."

Weston also said: ". . . the camera should be used for a recording of 'life,' for rendering the very substance and quintessence of the 'thing itself,' whether polished steel or palpitating flesh." In my creative work, I have strived for that end, producing a body of work which bears witness to the fiery intensity of Stevie Ray Vaughan's Stratocaster Licks, the sharp-edged architectural form of Houston's Transco Tower, or the phallic Gothic fantasy of the early Texas Commerce Bank building. Through my work, I try to show the correlation between science and spirituality, flesh and steel, wood and stone, emulsion and emotion.

This exhibition, *Delusional Architecture*, features interpretive photographs of Houston buildings and cityscapes, particularly buildings in the heart of the city and neighborhoods bordering Buffalo Bayou, such as Downtown and the Heights. Also included are photographs of musicians such as Stevie Ray Vaughan and Joe Ely, whose virtuosity has graced Houston stages for years.

Appropriately, the exhibition is installed in the Market Square Bar and Grill on Market Square in one of

Downtown's oldest buildings, dating from the late nineteenth century. It is one of the downtown businesses fighting to preserve Houston's cultural and architectural heritage in an uncertain age, but one that may also mark a new boom in the vitality of downtown Houston.

Tracy Hart

Stevie Ray Vaughan, 1987
Sam Houston Coliseum
Tracy Hart
Silver Gelatin Print

BRASIL CAFE GALLERY

INFERNO: Shopping In America by Warren Padula

I go shopping for the same reason other people go to horror movies: to see how scared I can get. I like to project half-remembered scenes from *Dawn of the Living Dead* onto the floor plan while I move as if by peristalsis through the large intestine of the shopping mall, feeling my vital signs oozing away while little infrared bar code sensors invisibly probe my wallet to check out what's left on my four major credit cards. Arnold Schwartzenegger generally runs by on the upper level about then, blasting people off the escalators with a two-hundred pound rocket gun. What I wouldn't give to have total control of the central sound system on, say, Easter Sunday!

I'm a bungee shopper: plunging into the bottomless abyss, gaining speed and entering zero gravity, going down past Dante, sometimes almost touching the promised ecstasy before being snapped back by the credit line.

The key to the psyche of shopping, the hieroglyphics of the whole business, can be read on the covers of the papers and magazines displayed at the checkout racks. From the checkout, you can watch the battle of false sunlight and deep shadow, of cheery self-improvement, dinner parties, and new products versus the new awful truth just proven Jesus really is living in El Paso, that our elected leaders are actually aliens, that we are all being watched by them. In this perfectly plausible alternate reality, the malls are space stations that have settled down on the outskirts of town, mother ships vacuuming up teenagers for conditioning. And why not? Someone besides ourselves should be held responsible.

Underneath the optimism of the daylight culture, a whole nightmare world is constantly bubbling. A world of rage and demons, frustration and fleeting satisfaction, wish fulfillment, and desire. Why is Apocalypse necessary? Because there's no easier resolution to the proliferation of monster babies, incurable epidemics, and public betrayals increasingly popping up through the mirror's surface and appearing in full daylight. The Wizard moved to Santa Monica leaving Oz on autopilot. He's in recovery now, but we are left in a laughing nightmare.

Outside in the parking lot, the car alarms are wailing. It's the outsiders again, driven mad by the sheer enormity of it all, snatching purses and stealing cars. Don't forget to lock your doors.

Warren Padula

Mouth, from the series *INFERNO: Shopping in America*, 1996
Warren Padula
Silver Gelatin Print

ALLO MOV ART SPACE

How's My Driving?
Mobile Exhibition

ARTISTS: BENEDIKTE FLORES ANSELL, SCOTT CALHOUN, CLAIRE CHAUVIN, ANDREA GROVER, LINDA HAYWARD, CHAD JOINER, JENNIE KING, TSUGUMI MAKI, PATRICK PHIPPS, JEFF SHORE, BILL WILLIS

This mobile art space was created by II multimedia artists who decorated the walls of the moving van. The project was designed to make three to four pit stops at various locations throughout Houston. In addition to our artwork, we include souvenir postcard reproductions of our work for sale. We describe this project as a deal on wheels.

Bennie Flores Ansell

PARTICIPATING SPACES NOT IN THE 1998 CATALOGUE

Ocotillo Gallery - Downtown, Market Square
MotherDog Studios - Downtown,
    NoHo Warehouse District
William Street Gallery - Downtown,
    NoHo Warehouse District
Nancy Worthington Gallery - Downtown,
    Commerce Street Warehouse District
Brent Gallery- Midtown/Third Ward
Mercedes Art Gallery - Midtown/Third Ward
Firehouse Gallery - Museum District
Holocaust Museum Houston- Museum District
Houston Museum of Natural Science -
    Museum District
Hyde Park Gallery - Museum District
L'Alliance Française - Museum District
Lawndale Art Center - Museum District
The Menil Collection - Museum District
Takara Gallery - Museum District
University of Texas Houston Health Science Center
    Medical School - Museum District
Benji's Restaurant - West University
Barbara Davis Gallery - Gallery Row, Colquitt
Hooks-Epstein Galleries, Inc. - Gallery Row, Colquitt
Great Hang-Up - Kipling/Upper Kirby
Koelsch Gallery - Kipling/Upper Kirby
Lowell Collins Gallery - Kipling/Upper Kirby
Casa Ramirez Folk Art Gallery - The Heights
Devin Borden Hiram Butler Gallery - The Heights
Rudolph Poissant Gallery - The Heights
Art Institute of Houston - Galleria Area
Paraiso Maravilla - Galleria Area
Story Sloan's Gallery - Galleria Area
Deutser Gallery, Jewish Community
    Center of Houston - Meyerland
Kim Son Restaurant - Downtown

LITERACY THROUGH PHOTOGRAPHY

It's more like a dance or the shift into the possible
with all that storms daily through the lives of
urban children.

Locking looking flat in chemicals set to fade into memory shelving to
hold time in it's passage.

A snake's slither, a trace of going—where do academics fit
into this awareness? And how to produce more connections,
one by one? Literate.

Visual and verbal mechanisms of what we tend to call higher thinking
skills—a real investment to life in Houston down the road.

This needs a prose connection: nine hundred and fifty kids,
mostly fifth and sixth graders, trained in creative writing and
visual literacy basics, toting loaded cameras in search of their lives.
Thinking it through, to pause and reach into appearances
(that heartbeat of our cultural discourse) and harvest scraps of
memory-heritage, history at the roots—constructions of identity
held in a moment for examination, investigation, and recombinant
imaging with pencil toward a philosophy of consciousness, a larger
cohesion of their wisdom.

It is more like welding.

David Brown

How do you educate students of today to be productive members of society in the year 2000 and beyond? What are the essential tools students need to participate in the next Industrial Revolution? Critical thinking skills, creativity, strategies of questioning, presentation skills, understanding of visual clues and cues, learning to learn, and to take responsibility for their own learning, all come to mind. To encourage the growth of these essential tools, FotoFest has developed the Literacy Through Photography (LTP) program by bringing together Wendy Ewald's Portraits and Dreams methods to help children photograph their lives and David Brown's innovative creative writing techniques for teaching literacy and writing skills. Their methodologies, along with the expertise of curriculum consultant Marie Scanlin, have produced the LTP curriculum guide.

LTP has been used in selected Houston Independent School District (HISD) elementary, middle, and high schools since 1990. Every year, FotoFest places a thousand cameras with film and processing in the classrooms and guides students and teachers through the process of discovery. Experience has shown that children's desires to communicate with a broader audience are heightened by discovering that they have something significant to express and contribute. Interest in refining their writing and presentation skills comes naturally when they know their work will be printed in anthologies and exhibited publicly on the *FotoFence*.

Advanced curriculum is being developed to be used in second-year LTP programs as well as new methodologies for integrating Literacy Through Photography with social science, math, language arts, and art classes. The Kaleidoscope School/Escuela Caleidoscopio is a new charter middle school featuring LTP. It is located at Cunningham Elementary School in southwest Houston. The Kaleidoscope School will serve as a professional and project development center for FotoFest's Literacy Through Photography visual literacy and writing program. The school will have a teacher training program that will directly address the goal of enhancing teacher knowledge, both for the school's own staff and for visiting teachers participating in workshops, internship opportunities, and classroom observation. Through the integration of core subjects, computers, and the LTP program, FotoFest's goal is to create self-motivated students who will continue to learn for the rest of their lives.

David Brown and Marie Scanlin
Literacy Through Photography
FotoFest

The Literacy Through Photography program and the FotoFence received special support from Fuji Photo Film USA, CANON USA Inc., Fuji Color Processing, Houston Endowment Inc., William Stamps Farish Foundation, Favrot Fund, Harris and Eliza Kempner Fund, Powell Foundation, and the City of Houston and the Texas Commission on the Arts through the Cultural Arts Council of Houston/Harris County.

My best friend, Jeannie, the one who had the greatest impact on my career goals, took this picture of me. It shows how determined I am to reach those goals. To further illustrate this, I am even positioning my hands in the way I would hold my Emmy Award.

REBECCA CONNORS, RISING STAR!

The intensity in the room is unbearable as this year's host slowly opens the envelope. "And the winner of this year's Best Actress Emmy Award is . . . " Everyone is sitting on the edge of their chairs, but simultaneously trying to keep their composure as the drum roll makes time seem to stand still, " . . . Rebecca Connors!"

This scene replays itself constantly through all my waking hours. I hear those words aloud and booming at the world, echoing to far distances, letting everyone know I fulfilled my life-long dream.

Ever since I can remember, I've been interested in acting. But, my interest was only mild until my best friend and I and a few others entered a talent show and performed a skit we had written ourselves. It wasn't the first play I'd been in, but it just made something inside me click; from then on I've been hooked. I try out for any part in any play I can. I even got a part in a movie! It is an independent film. Nevertheless, it is a start.

In this picture I am wearing a 1950's dress which exhibits the side of me that likes and appreciates the 50's era. Also, I am wearing long, silky black gloves and an elegant diamond necklace. This is an outfit I would definitely wear to receive such an award. In the background are black and white photos of old famous movie stars, again from the 50's.

This is my favorite picture of me. It depicts so much about my personality that most people have never known. Most of all, I love how it shows my dedication to becoming a wonderful actress.

Rebecca Connors
Milby High School
November 5, 1997

MY BEAUTIFUL BED

My pillow is full of dreams, memories, secrets and love. My palace of dreams I have dreamed. My secrets are hidden under my white blankets and the pillow is filled with little flowers, floating memories. My purple and brown blanket keeps me warm. I have had it since I was in the fourth grade. It's name is Webbles. The creamy brown, purple, blue lines are like lightening falling from the sky. There's a little white lost between the colors. My blue sky and dark blue blankets are warm. The dark blue blankets and little dots in groups of 3s, 2s, 4s and 5s. My body has been lying down on tired days. My bed is a secret world for life. My future, past and present life will or has slept, rested and dreamed eternity.

My white, soft pillow will stay soft forever. My bed is a body covered with her dress. My bed is a representative of love from my dad. He gave it to me with love on my ninth birthday. My purple backpack is under my bed. My bed has little wrinkles. My bed has the shape of a big building. The small sticks that are poles represent six wishes. Every wish I will wish will come true. They are my presents from my magical castle. I won't waste my wishes on something that I would regret for life. I will wish a wish for every problem that I have. My wishes will come true if I believe they will.

My bed, my bed, My Beautiful Bed is a light in life. It shines every morning, every afternoon and every night like a star in every day of life. I say this with love, with heart and feelings within my blood. It shines, it shines. It gives me power for wishes to come true. My bed is soft like magical clouds floating in the air. My bed is as white as an angel. I'm the wings supporting my bed like winds support the bird's body. It's flying away in a place that problems don't exist. I'm like them, a dreamer flying into heaven. My bed is a clock ticking. You hear the tick-tock in your mind. It is telling me love, love. This is My Beautiful Bed, My Beautiful Bed.

Joanna Carreño
Kaleidoscope School

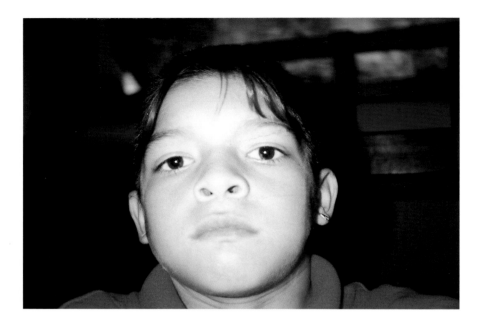

MY SELF-PORTRAIT

I like to be with my family. They always take me to the park. I always eat fish and shrimp. The shrimp tastes like chicken. My family is very nice to me. They are real cool.

My school is really interesting. It has a lot of contests and one time I won. I hope I win this one. I like my teacher. She is really cool and teaches us how to do all our work. I hope she knows that she is a good teacher to me and my classmates. She is really nice to me.

In my future, I want to be a policeman. Police are real cool to me and that's why I want to be a policeman. I am going to go all the way to college. I really hope I am going to make it. I know it is hard to graduate, but who cares? I am going to make it all the way. My favorite high school is Milby. I hope we all get to graduate. I like the way i act in school. My favorite subject is math. I can do math and day and night. I also like the way that i always have a reason to be mad or sad. I hope that we will see each other forever.

Cesar Jaure
Fifth Grade
Southmayd Elementary

MY DADDY

My daddy is filled with beautiful flowers.
I feel good because I know that he loves to
    work with nature.
He is wearing his favorite blue shirt.
I know that he will still like it and want it when
    years pass.
He likes green; that is why he is surrounded by green.
He likes green because it's what he has done for
    work since he was 19 years old.
He is wearing a cap, colored green.
He wears a green cap every day because it covers
    him from the sun.
My daddy is planting flowers in pots.
When he is putting flowers in the pots he looks
    like he is helping the flowers live.
He bends down on his knee.
When he is bent down on his knee he looks like a frog.
The sun shines right on him.
When the sun gives him light it looks like
    he is a wonderful daddy.
The tree gives him a little shade.
The tree is like hands waving at him and
    giving air for him to be pleased.
In front of him there are seven orange pots.
The seven pots filled with flowers look like
    pots filled with gold.
My daddy loves nature.
When Daddy works with the lawn mower
    cutting the grass, it's like he is cutting his hair.
There is little grass shown.
But in real life there is more than that.

Maricela Mendoza
Cunningham Elementary

A PIECE OF WORK

I am standing on the garage my father made with his own hands. He had to build it two different times after he bought our house. The first time he made it was fine but about fifteen years later he needed to build the top because he did not like it anymore. The old sheet metal and the wood was rusted, so he made it all over again. I helped him build the top and I am wearing a jersey that just recently came out. It is a Drexler jersey. The Jordan shoes that i am wearing, I paid for with my own money.

I always have to work very hard for my money. Those shoes were $97.41 that I saved up from cutting the grass each week. I got $100.00 for cutting the grass and if I go working with my dad on Saturdays, but only for a half day, I will get paid $20.00. When I helped my dad with the top of the roof, we always had trouble with the branch on the left. It was always hitting me in the head. With my shoes, I got red and black laces that go with the colors on my shoes. On the right of the photograph, the cable TV cord was always in the way too. Also, I have my hair combed back. I used to have it combed to the side but now I comb it back. I chose this photograph as my favorite because it reminds me of the hard work that I have done.

Jesus Deleon
Sixth Grade
McReynolds Middle School

MY SISTER BROOKE

My sister Brooke is 4 months old. She is very neat to have around. She makes me laugh when I am sad and glad to be a big brother.

Brooke was born on July 14, 1997 and that is two days after my birth day. I like to think of her as the best present I could have gotten for my birthday. Brand new, she weighed 7 pounds and 3 ounces. She out-weighed me by one ounce. Now, she weighs over 15 pounds. Boy, is she greedy.

I have been the only child for years. When my parents told me we were expecting a baby, I was in a state of shock. Do not get me wrong, I was very excited. Some people thought I would be mad or jealous of the new baby in the family, but i am not. I think of her as a blessing. In time, I just hope she feels the same way about me.

Each day I can not wait for school to end. I miss seeing her through the day. Some times in class, I sit and wonder what she could be doing at that moment. My grandmother takes care of her while we are away. I know she is being well taken care of, but I still miss her. Brooke is very special to me and I would not want her to be mistreated. My mom and dad say we look a lot alike as babies. I do not think we look alike. She is cute and cuddly. When she cries, I feel like crying, also. To be honest, I cried for Brooke when I was told she was in a car accident a few weeks ago. She was not injured but the thought of the whole experience she went through scared me. She is the only sister I have.

She has grown a lot in these past 4 months. So far, she laughs aloud, tries to sit alone, holds her head up, baby talks and recognizes us. I can not wait for her to crawl., then walk. When I hold her, my arms get tired fast. Besides, holding her gives me a shirt wet with drool. But it is okay, she is my sister—Brooke.

Andre Darden
Black Middle School

UNTITLED

One of my best friends is my bookshelf. It has all the things I love to read. My bookshelf has it all—fiction and nonfiction. The colors of the books make me feel as colorful as a rainbow. Books and colors make me feel as happy as a clown. That is why I took this picture!

I took this picture with a Mickey Mouse balloon because he is my favorite Disney character. When my older sister was about to push the button, we noticed something very strange. She was just about to take the picture when everything started tilting and falling. We had no idea what was going on! I remained calm through all this commotion. My eyes got bigger than a lizard's because of all the moving and shaking, but still I remained calm. It was a very scary sight. My baby brother was in his crib and it started trotting around the room. We waited no more. My sister took the pic-

ture at once and then we ran to get the furniture and save it from destruction. Once the house stopped moving and shaking, we went back to our normal lives. We tried to figure out what happened that day, but we never did.

Azucena Flores
Fifth grade Crespo Elementary

MY GRANDMA AND MY PARENTS

My mom is on the right hand side of my grandma. My dad is on the other side. My grandma is in the middle sitting in a chair. They were at my brother's house. It was my sister-in-law's brother's birthday. I love this picture because it shows love. And also, because the faces show some kind of triangle and my grandma is laughing. It looks like my dad is serious. I don't know why but I think because it is 10:00. I really really like taking pictures at night because it looks very pretty. Plus, it gives darker shades to the clothes instead of very light colors. Also, you can't see the cars driving past on the street or people walking down the sidewalk.

Last Christmas, my brother invited dad, mom, my sister, and me to Acapulco. My sister and I told mom and dad to say yes. We were so excited, we wanted the days to go past very fast.

I choose this picture because my grandma was here for a visit. I wanted to get her in a picture with my parents and I knew she was leaving after Christmas. I was sleepy when I took this picture. I took it and that is why I am not in it.

Yvette Martinez
Sixth grade Deady Middle School

ARTISTS

ARTIST BIOGRAPHIES

BENEDIKTE FLORES ANSELL
Born in 1967 in Manila, Philippines, Ansell has resided in the U.S. since early childhood. She is an imagemaker who uses mixed-media techniques to explore racial and cultural identity. Ansell attended the University of South Florida for her B.A. in photography and is currently an M.F.A. candidate at the University of Houston. Her work has been exhibited in group shows, including the Arlington Museum of Art in Arlington, Texas and Diverseworks Artspace in Houston.

NOBUYOSHI ARAKI
Currently living and working in his native city of Tokyo, Japanese photographer Araki first attracted attention in 1970 with the first of his many publications, *Sentimental Journeys*. This work chronicled, through explicit photos, Araki's honeymoon with his young bride, Yoko. Araki has continued his "voyeuristic" eye, capturing gritty urban images of nightlife in Tokyo's "red light" district. His most publicized body of work contains images of Japanese women in carefully choreographed states of bondage. Araki's photography has been the subject of over 130 books. His work has been featured in museum exhibitions throughout Europe, Japan, and the United States and was included in the 1995 *Carnegie International*.

GRZEGORZ BANASZKIEWICZ
Born in 1951, Czestochowa, Poland, Banaszkiewicz received his M.F.A. from the Academy of Fine Arts in Krakow. His media are printmaking, drawing, and photography. Banaszkiewicz' graphic work, as well as his drawings, has roots in photography. In 1996 he was invited by the Royal Academy in Antwerp, Belgium, to teach the technique of heliogravure. Since 1976 he has exhibited in Poland and has participated in sixty major international exhibitions. Banaszkiewicz is a recipient of numerous awards in the fields of printmaking and photography. His works are included in the permanent collections of the Museum of Modern Art, Lodz, Poland; the National Library, Warsaw, Poland; and the Kunsthalle, Nuremberg, Germany, among others.

CRAIG J. BARBER
Barber received his B.A. in photography from State University New York. He has participated in numerous group exhibitions, including *PHOTOKINA* in Cologne, Germany and Tel-Aviv, Israel; *Faculty Exhibition* at the International Center of Photography in New York; and, most recently, *Beaux Arts* at the Dallas Museum of Art. Barber has also shown work in a number of one-person shows. He has won several grants and awards and has published work in *Shots*, *Photographer's Forum*, *View Camera*, and *Photo Metro*. Barber has served as instructor and guest lecturer at several colleges and universities and has been the subject of many articles. He is represented in public collections in Russia and the United States.

OLIVO BARBIERI
Born in 1954 in Carpi (Modena), Italy, Barbieri started photographing in 1971, while studying pedagogics at the University of Bologna and, simultaneously, at *D.A.M.S.* During those years he intensified his interest in photography, in particular carrying out research in color and industrial landscape. Barbieri has been active in the developments of contemporary Italian photography. Since the early 1980s, he has been taking part in the most important campaigns of territorial documentation in Italy, including *Viaggio in Italia*, *La Via Emilia*, and *Progetto Beni Architettonici e Ambientali della Provincia di Milano*. He has participated in many solo and group exhibitions and is the subject of numerous monographs.

LAURA BARRÓN ECHAURI
Born in 1966 in Mexico City, Barrón earned her degree in visual arts at the Escuela Nacional de Artes Plásticas at the Universidad Nacional Autónoma de México in 1992. She has collaborated in publications, set design, television, and multimedia projects. Barrón has given lectures and workshops in photography as well as taught private classes. In 1996, she received a scholarship for young artists in photography from Fondo Nacional para la Cultura y las Artes. She has participated in four solo and more than fifteen group exhibitions. Barrón is currently working on a project at a digital imaging studio at Centro Multimedia at the Centro Nacional de las Artes in Mexico City.

GERALDO DE BARROS
Born in 1923 in Xavantes, São Paulo, Brazil, de Barros currently lives and works in São Paulo. He is a painter, industrial designer, and photographer. De Barros studied under Max Bill at the Hochschule für Gestaltung in Ulm, Germany in 1951. His solo exhibitions include *Photoforms*, Museu de Arte de São Paulo, 1950; *Concrete Art*, Zurich, 1960; *Brazilian Construction Design in Art*, Pinacoteca do Estado de São Paulo, 1977; Venice, 1979; *Brazilians and Their Cultural Roots*, Museu de Arte de São Paulo, 1980; and *Tradition and Rupture*, Fundação Bienal de São Paulo, 1984.

UTA BARTH
Born in 1958 in Germany. Currently lives and works in Los Angeles. Barth's work has been the subject of numerous shows, including exhibitions at the Museum of Contemporary Art, Los Angeles; the Museum of Contemporary Art, Chicago; the Addison Gallery of American Art, Andover, Massachusetts; ACME Gallery, Santa Monica; Tanya Bonakdar Gallery, New York; Andehn-Schiptjenko, Stockholm; London Projects, London; Rena Bransten Gallery, San Francisco; and S. L. Simpson Gallery, Toronto. Barth's work has also been included in group exhibitions at such venues as the Museum of Contemporary Art, New York; the Museum of Contemporary Art, Miami; Rooseum Center for Contemporary Art, Malmo, Sweden; Los Angeles County Museum of Art; Parco Gallery, Tokyo; De Appel Foundation, Amsterdam; Wexner Center for the Arts, Columbus, Ohio; Armand Hammer Museum of Art, Los Angeles; and the Museum of Contemporary Photography, Chicago.

GABRIELE BASILICO
Born in 1944 in Milan, Basilico holds a degree in architecture and for many years has been one of Italy's best-known photographers. In fifteen years of working as a professional photographer for the industrial and publishing sectors, he has continued to cultivate his personal photographic interests. The products of this private exploration, concentrated chiefly on the themes of architecture and the urban landscape, have been shown in numerous solo and group exhibitions in Italy and abroad. As well as contributing photographs to numerous publications, Basilico has published *Dancing in Emilia*, 1980; *Milano Architecture 1919-1939*, 1985; *Italia & France*, 1986; and *Vedute*, 1987.

XIMENA BERECOCHEA FERNANDEZ
A freelance photographer since 1992, Berechochea has exhibited work at Centro de la Imagen, Mexico City; Centro de Investigación de Historia y Sociedad, Galería Nacho López, Veracruz, Mexico; Centro de Arte Moderno in Guadalajara; *Segundo Salón de Fotografía*, Veracruz, Mexico; and Museo de Arte Moderno INBA, among others. She has published work in several publications in Mexico, Austria, and Spain. In 1995, Berecochea won a scholarship for young artists in photography from Fondo Nacional para la Cultura y las Artes.

CHARLES BIASINY-RIVERA
Biasiny-Rivera is cofounder and executive director of En Foco, Inc., a nonprofit visual arts agency in New York since 1973. He has been a photographer and curator for over twenty years, and he served an apprenticeship with Sir Cecil Beaton from 1960 to 1964. Biasiny-Rivera's own photographic work has been widely exhibited and published. He is also known for his pioneering work in the promotion of Latino and African-American photographic artists. Biasiny-Rivera has curated a number of important shows in Puerto Rican photography, such as *Island Journey* (1995-96) and the Puerto Rican section of *American Voices* (1994-97). He is publisher of *Nueva Luz* and he has been a panelist for the visual arts program of the New York State Council on the Arts (1992).

HARROD BLANK
Harrod resides in Berkley, California and earned a B.A. in theatre arts/film in 1986 from the University of California at Santa Cruz. There, he created his first art car *Oh My God*. This led to his national exploration for, and photography of, other art cars and their creators. His documentary film *Wild Wheels* was completed and self-distributed in 1992, and PBS has since broadcast the film nationally. The companion book, *Wild Wheels*, was published in 1993 and named "Best Book for Young Adults" by the American Library Association. Combining his passion for car art and his love for photography, Blank attached 1,705 cameras to his van and calls it the *Camera Van*. Ten of these cameras work, giving Blank the ability to photograph the public's candid reactions. Currently he is at work on a book of these reaction shots to be titled *I've Got a Vision*, and a 30-minute documentary titled *Driving the Dream for National Geographic Explorer*. He plans to expand *Driving the Dream* into the feature length sequel of *Wild Wheels*, scheduled to be completed in the fall of 1998.

SUZANNE BLOOM AND ED HILL (MANUAL)
Since 1985 Bloom and Hill have been working in digital media, manipulating photographs, and creating installations and interactive computer programs for museums and galleries. They contemplate the vicissitudes of nature and cyberculture in their electronic studios in Vermont and in Texas, where both have been professors of art at the University of Houston for twenty-one years. Their work has been exhibited widely throughout this country and abroad and is included in the collections of the Museum of Contemporary Photography, the Los Angeles County Museum of Art, and the International Museum of Photography, among others. Their current projects include producing electronic art for a new wastewater testing facility being built by the City of Houston, maintaining a Web site for digital imaging, and developing an eccentric approach to the pastoral landscape.

AMALIA BLYTH
Born in Phoenix, Arizona, Blyth received her education at the University of Central England and the Bournville College of Art in England. Heavily influenced by "fringe subcultures", Blyth completed large bodies of work involving the punk subculture in the United Kingdom, including *Identity*, a detailed study of the bands the Dead Kennedys and Black Flag, and *Release*, a series of portraits examining English punks. Her photographs of the low-rider culture can be seen in the book *Art Cars: Revolutionary Movement*. Blyth currently resides in New York.

SANDRA BORDIN
Born in 1961 in Santa Maria, Rio Grande do Sul, Brazil, Bordin lived and worked in Porto Alegre and currently resides in New York City. She graduated in visual communications from the University of Santa Maria in 1985. Bordin exhibited her color series *Slaughter: Insistent Dream* at the *V Coloquio Latinoamericano de Fotografía* in Mexico City and at the *International Biennal of Photography* of Curitiba in 1996. She is represented by Throckmorton Fine Arts, New York.

KATYA BRAILOWSKY PLATA
Brailowsky earned a Bachelor's degree in philosophy and arts at Sarah Lawrence College in 1990 and a degree in photojournalism at the International Center for Photography in New York in 1994. She has worked as an archives assistant for Magnum photo agency in New York and as workshop assistant at Centro de la Imagen, Mexico City. Brailowsky exhibited work at *Fotoseptiembre 1996* in a solo show called *Aeropuerto*. In 1997 she won a photography scholarship for young artists from Fondo Nacional para la Cultura y las Artes.

ADRIANA CALATAYUD MORÁN
Born in 1967 in Mexico City, Calatayud earned her Bachelor's degree in graphic communications at Escuela Nacional de Artes Plásticas in 1988. She has participated in several solo and group exhibitions, including *Fotoseptiembre*, Mexico City; *Seventh International Exhibition of Artistic Photography in China*; *Fifth Art Triennial in Majdanek '94*, Poland; and *Århus Festival*, Women's Museum, Denmark. In 1996, Calatayud won a scholarship for young artists in photography from Fondo Nacional para la Cultura y las Artes.

SCOTT CALHOUN
Calhoun is a devout Jungian who lives and works in Tokyo, New York, and Amsterdam.

JAN CAMP
Camp was born in 1946. She has participated in many solo and group exhibitions, including *Glancing Back*, Oakland, California; *Reflections from Mid Life*, Tulsa, Oklahoma; *Five Women Photographers*, Madrid, New Mexico; and *Visual AIDS*, Museum of Contemporary Arts, Baltimore, Maryland. She has won the MacDowell Colony Artist Residency, the San Francisco Business Arts Council's Arts Leadership Initiative Award, and a College of Santa Fe Visual Art Scholarship, among others. Camp is represented in public collections and is the subject of a number of articles. She is a member of Friends of Photography and president of Iris Arts and Educational Group, Inc., Berkely, California.

KATHLEEN CAMPBELL
Campbell earned an M.F.A. degree in photography at the University of New Mexico in 1994. She has an extensive career as a photographer, lecturer, curator, and writer who has exhibited work in numerous venues, including the Houston Center for Photography, the Guadalupe Cultural Arts Center in San Antonio, Texas, and the University of New Mexico Art Museum. Campbell has won many honors and awards, including a National Endowment for the Arts internship (1985-86), a Nuala McGann Drescher award (1994), and a New York State Council on the Arts curatorial grant (1995). She has published photographic and written work in several publications, including *Number: An Independent Quarterly of the Visual Arts*, *Photo-Metro*, *Art Papers*, and the *San Francisco Camerawork Quarterly*.

PAUL CAPONIGRO
Born 1932 in Boston, Caponigro encountered photography around 1952, while studying the piano at Boston University. He was drafted in 1953 and was stationed as a photographer in San Francisco, where he met and studied with Benjamin Chin. After his service tour, he became the protégé of, and later assistant to, Minor White. His first one-person exhibition was held at George Eastman House in 1955. Caponigro's distinguished career has included the publication of five monographs and three limited-edition portfolios of original prints. Grants from the Guggenheim Foundation and the National Endowment for the Arts have helped support his work in the British Isles, France, and Japan. His work has appeared in periodicals such as *Art in America*, *Contemporary Photographer*, and the *Saturday Review*. His photographs are in many collections, including the Philadelphia Museum of Art, George Eastman House, and the Museum of Modern Art.

KEITH CARTER
Internationally recognized as a photographer and educator, Carter has exhibited and collected widely. He is the author of five previously published monographs: *From Uncertain to Blue*, 1988; *The Blue Man*, 1990; *Mole*, 1992; *Heaven of Animals*, 1995; and *Bones*, 1996. His latest book, *Keith Carter Photographs: Twenty-Five Years*, was published in 1997 by the University of Texas Press in collaboration with the Wittliff Collection of Southwestern and Mexican Photography.

VINCENZO CASTELLA
Born in 1952 in Naples, Castella currently lives in Milano. He began photographing in 1975 after completing his studies at the University of Rome. Castella has published his work extensively. He has participated in numerous exhibitions and is represented in various public and private collections.

CLAIRE CHAUVIN
Born in 1971 in Corpus Christi, Texas, Chauvin lived most of her life overseas as an expatriate. She moved to Houston in 1988 where she completed her B.F.A. and M.F.A. degrees in photography at the University of Houston. Her photographs, which are produced digitally, explore the link between art and science and technology, as well as the ambiguous territory between them.

ALAIN GERARD CLEMENT
Born in 1945 in Balesmes, France, Clement has lived and worked in Houston since 1978. He received grants from the National Endowment for the Arts in 1988 and the Cultural Arts Council of Houston in 1986-87. He has shown work throughout New York, Texas, Canada, Scandinavia, and his native France. Clement's work in the photogram technique succeeded that of Man Ray, Laszlo Maholy-Nagy, and Floris Neussis as he created landscapes and tableaux using the process. For the last four years he has worked with photogenic drawing, a technique perfected by him.

ROCHELLE COSTI
Born in 1961 in Caxias do Sul, Rio Grande do Sul, Brazil, Costi currently lives and works in São Paulo. She graduated with a degree in social communications from the Catholic University of Rio Grande do Sul in 1981 and studied graphic design at Escola Guignard in 1982. In 1983 She was awarded first prize at the *International Biennal of Photographic Art*, São Paulo. Costi has exhibited widely in Brazil and abroad. She is also a film and video artist.

EUGÈNE (EUGENIO) COURRET
Born in Angoulême, France, Courret arrived in Perú in 1860 and worked as a photographer in the studio of Eugène Mauseury. In 1863, he and his brother opened their own studio named Fotografía Central. The Courret studio won a gold medal at the *Exposición Industrial de Lima* in 1869 and again in 1872. At that time, the Courret brothers won the exclusive rights to photograph the events and infrastructure of the exposition. After several years of owning various studios and name changes, the Courret brothers retained one studio and renamed it E. Courret y Cía. In 1900, the studio won the gold medal at the *Exposition Universale de París*.

DICK CRAIG
Born in 1952 in Mexico City, Craig graduated from the University of Houston. His art and photography have been featured in exhibitions around the country, including *Holidays and Festivals in America* at the Balch Institute for Ethnic Studies in Philadelphia and *A Glimpse of Central America* at CARECEN in Houston. Craig's photographs have garnered honors in competitions such as the 1996 Art Car Photography Open and the International Photography Competition at the Institute de Bellas Artes in San Miguel de Allende, Mexico. Craig currently resides in Houston.

MARCO ANTONIO CRUZ LÓPEZ

Born in 1957 in Puebla, Mexico, López began his career as a photojournalist in the late 1970s. Since then, he has collaborated in major Mexican newspaper publications and in foreign publications such as *Life*, *Stern*, and *París Match*. He has produced over thirty photographic documentaries and essays and is editor of *Contra la Pared: Violencia en la Ciudad de México* (1993) and *Cafetaleros: Trabajadores Indígenas del Café en el Estado de Chiapas* (1996). López is currently editing the essay *Ciegos* with Casa de las Imágenes. His work has earned many awards in Mexico. He has participated in both solo and group exhibitions in Mexico as well as abroad. López is currently director of the photo agency Imagenlatina, headquartered in Mexico City.

VALDIR CRUZ

Cruz made a full-time commitment to his career as a professional photographer in 1984. As a result of studying with George Tice for two years, he has printed exhibitions for Tice and limited editions for the Estate of Edward Steichen, among others. Since 1982, Cruz has been building the *Guarapuava* series, a major body of work in progress revolving around life in his hometown. His portrait essay of a neo-Gothic cathedral in Curitiba, Brazil has been published in book form under the title *Catedral Basílica de Nossa Senhora da Luz dos Pinhais*. Cruz' work has been widely exhibited and collected internationally, including the Museum of Modern Art in New York and the Museum of Fine Arts, Houston. He was awarded a 1996 fellowship by the John Simon Guggenheim Foundation for the third phase of his current project, *Faces of the Rainforest*.

EDGAR LADRÓN DE GUEVARRA

De Guevarra was born in 1961 in Mexico City. He has participated in a number of solo exhibitions, including Solo Exhibit in Mexico City and Bucharest, *Intimidad* in *Fotoseptiembre 94* in Mexico City, and *The Irish in New York* at the Museum of the City of New York, as well as in group exhibitions, including *La Memoria del Tiempo* at the Museo de Arte Moderno and *VIII Photography Biennial* at Centro de la Imagen, in Mexico City. De Guevarra was won several grants, including a grant from the National Council for the Arts and Culture (FONCA) for young creators and a Fulbright grant for an M.F.A. at the School of Visual Arts in New York.

MARIANNA DELLEKAMP

Born in 1968 in Mexico City, Dellekamp joined the board of directors of Consejo Mexicano de Fotografía in 1995 and became editor of that organization's magazine, *Sin Título*. She has conducted workshops and assisted in the direction and coordination of wardrobe and costume for television commercials. Dellekamp has participated in a number of exhibitions and has published work in newspapers and catalogues, as well as produced picture postcards. Dellekamp is represented in the collections of Centro de la Imagen in Mexico City and Instituto Cultural de Aguascalientes.

JESSE DEMARTINO

In 1996 DeMartino received a B.A. in art and English from Rice University, where he studied photography under Geoff Winningham. Twice named to the Golden Light Awards list of Top 100 Photographers, he won second place in the Santa Fe Center for Visual Arts 1997 International Project competition. Recently, DeMartino received a fellowship from the Houston Center for Photography for his project on skateboarders. He has shown work in over thirty exhibitions in a dozen states and has been featured in *Shots* magazine and *Creative Camera*. DeMartino's work is represented in the Museum of Fine Arts, Houston.

CARLOS DÍAZ

Born in 1951 in Pontiac, Michigan. Díaz currently resides in Brighten, Michigan. After obtaining a B.F.A. degree from the Center for Creative Studies, he earned an M.F.A. degree from the University of Michigan. He is currently chairman of the photography department at the Center for Creative Studies in Detroit, Michigan, where he has taught for fifteen years. He worked previously as a designer, draftsman, and graphic artist for engineering and research companies. Díaz has received grants from the National Endowment for the Arts, the Ford Foundation, Arts Midwest, Polaroid Corporation, and the Michigan Council for the Arts. His work has been shown in Central America, Europe, and throughout the United States.

DORNITH DOHERTY

Born in Houston, Texas, Doherty is associate professor of photography at the University of North Texas. She received her B.A. in Spanish and French language and literature from Rice University and her M.F.A. from Yale University. Doherty has received several fellowships, including a William J. Fulbright Lecture/Research Fellowship and a Society for Contemporary Photography Fellowship. She has had solo, two-person, and group shows in the United States and in Mexico. Doherty's photographs are included in the collections of the Museum of Fine Arts, Milwaukee, the Minneapolis Institute of Arts, and the Museum of Fine Arts, Houston, among others.

GEORGE DUREAU

Born in 1930 in New Orleans, Dureau studied at Louisiana State University in Baton Rouge and the School of Architecture at Tulane University in New Orleans. He works in New Orleans as a painter, draftsman, and photographer. Dureau has exhibited work in New York, Paris, London, and New Orleans. His photographs have been widely published, and in a monograph was produced in 1986 with an introduction by Edward Lucie-Smith.

PÍA ELIZONDO

Born in 1963 in Mexico City, Elizondo studied at the Facultad de Filosofía y Letras at the Universidad Nacional Autónoma de México before becoming a self-taught photographer. She has participated in more than sixteen group exhibitions, including *Fotografía Mexicana*, Madrid; *En las Calles*, Hammond Galleries, Lancaster, Ohio; and *Hecho en México: Una selección de arte mexicano contemporáneo*, Galería El Museo, Bogotá. Elizondo has also exhibited work in solo exhibitions in Mexico and Brazil. She has published work in magazines, catalogues, newspapers, and books. In 1994, she won a scholarship for young artists in photography from Fondo Nacional para la Cultura y las Artes.

GARY FAYE

Born in Colorado in 1938, Faye currently resides in Houston. He received his B.F.A. from the Art Center of Design, Los Angeles. For a year in the late 1970s he worked as an assistant to Ansel Adams at his Yosemite Workshop and has led many workshops since. Faye's work has been exhibited extensively throughout America and is included in many private and public collections including the Museum of Fine Arts, Houston.

VALENTIN GERTSMAN

Born in Moscow in 1925, Dr. Gertsman was a respected orthopedic surgeon in Russia, and has continued in the medical field since immigrating to Houston in 1974. Gertsman's introduction to photography occurred almost by accident in 1980, when he began photographing his driftwood sculptures. His sensitive eye, curiosity, and surgical background enable him to see objects from a special perspective. As a surgeon with his instruments, Gertsman is able to restore and create new life out of architectural elements with his camera. His photocompositions appear in various magazines and have been displayed in art galleries, museums, and public spaces worldwide. Two works were recently acquired by the Tretyakov State Gallery in Moscow.

LUIGI GHIRRI

Ghirri was born in 1943 in Scandiano (Reggio Emilia), Italy. He began photographing in 1970 and, soon after, participated in his first exhibition in Modena. Since then, he has exhibited and published work extensively in Italy and abroad. Ghirri has published numerous articles and texts on photography, including *Capri*, a book on Italian architecture and landscape, 1983; *Aldo Rossi*, 1987; and *Fenici a Palazzo Grassi*, 1988.

MAYA GODED COLICHIO

Born in 1967 in Mexico City, Goded studied photography at Escuela Activa de Fotografía, Consejo Mexicano de Fotografía, and Centro de la Imagen in Mexico City and at the International Center of Photography in New York. She has participated in a number of solo and group exhibitions in Mexico, Europe, and the United States. Goded has published work in *Tierra Negra*, a book funded by Fondo Nacional para la Cultura y las Artes, Instituto Nacional Indigenista y Culturas Populares.

MARUCH SANTÍZ GÓMEZ

Santíz was born in 1975 in San Juan Chamula, Chiapas, Mexico. She has worked professionally as a photographer in Mexico, the United States, and South Africa. Santíz' current project *Creencias de Chamula*, which will be on exhibit at *FotoFest 98*, is scheduled for publication. Since 1993 she is a member of the Asociación Tzotzil-Tzeltal for writers and actors in Chiapas. Santíz has acted in puppet and theater productions in Mexico, the United States, and Honduras, and has published a number of written works. She is a member of the Archivo Fotográfico Indígena de Ciesas-Sureste, from which she received a grant to study anthropology in Chiapas.

CLAUDETTE CHAMPBRUN GOUX

Born in Algeria, Goux is French and presently resides in Houston. With early training in philosophy and sociology, she will receive her B.F.A. in photography from Rice University in 1997. Goux works in both color and black and white and has worked on projects as diverse as places of worship in Houston, French people, and details of landscape in Texas. Her work has been exhibited in two solo shows as well as in numerous juried exhibitions.

MILTON H. GREENE

Greene was born in 1922 in New York and began taking pictures at the age of fourteen. He apprenticed himself to the photojournalist Elliot Eliosofen and later worked as an assistant to the fashion photographer Louise Dahl-Wolfe. During the 1950s and 1960s, Greene's work appeared in major national publications, including *Vogue*, *Bazaar*, *Life*, and *McCalls*. His portraits of artists, musicians, and film, television, and theatrical celebrities include Marilyn Monroe, Grace Kelly, Sammy Davis, Jr., Alfred Hitchcock, Queen Elizabeth, Paul Newman, and Dizzy Gillespie. Greene's photographs, prints, and posters have been exhibited in major museums and galleries throughout the world, including the Chicago Art Institute, Museé de Marais (Paris), Nikon House, and the International Center for Photography (New York). His work has been published in many books, including *The First Fifty Years of Life*, Time-Life Books; *My Story—Marilyn Monroe*, Stein & Day; and *Of Women and Their Elegance*, a collaboration with Norman Mailer and Simon & Schuster.

KIMBERLY GREMILLION

Born in Chicago, Gremillion resides in Houston. Within the past year, she has had seven solo exhibitions, including shows in Houston at the Children's Museum, the Houston Grand Opera, and the Alley Theater. Gremillion is scheduled for solo shows in 1998 at Women & Their Work in Austin, Wyndy Morehead Gallery in New Orleans, Macon and Company in Atlanta, and the Galveston Arts Center. Last summer, she was featured in *Photo Metro* magazine. Gremillion is represented in numerous collections, including the Museum of Fine Arts, Houston; the Hertzberg Circus Museum in San Antonio; the Dancing Bear Collection (W. M. Hunt, New York); and the Harry Ransom Humanities Research Center at the University of Texas, Austin. She is currently working on *Dark Edges*, a book of circus images. She is represented by Ricco-Maresca Gallery in New York.

ANDREA GROVER

Born in 1970 on Long Island, New York, Grover attended Syracuse University for her B.F.A. and the School of the Art Institute of Chicago for her M.F.A. She recently completed her two-year tenure as a core fellow at the Glassell School of Art at the Museum of Fine Arts, Houston. She is a visual artist who works in traditional and electronic media. Her short film, *Rubbernecking* (co-produced with Patrick Walsh), was an official selection for the 1997 Cinema Texas Filmfest at the University of Texas, Austin. Grover was featured by Elga Wimmer Gallery, New York at the *1997 Expoarte Guadalajara* in Mexico. She is presently an adjunct professor of art at Texas Southern University in Houston.

HARRY GRUYAERT

Gruyaert was born in 1941 in Anvers, Belgium. He studied at the Brussels School of Film and Television and, after graduation, worked in the fashion and advertising industries in Paris. This experience complemented Gruyaert's work as director of photography in several films produced for Flemish television. In 1972 he photographed the Olympic Games in Munich, as well as the first flight of the Apollo space mission. Gruyaert received first prize from the Kodak Critic's Choice in 1976 for his photographs of Morocco. He joined the Magnum photo agency in 1981 and, three years later, received a research and development grant from the French Minister of Culture for a photography project on India. Gruyaert has published several books, including *White Lights* (1990) and *Morocco* (1990).

GUIDO GUIDI

Born in 1941 in Cesena, Italy, Guidi studied architecture at the University Institute of Architecture and at the Higher Course in Industrial Design in Venice. Since 1970, he has worked at the University Institute of Architecture and since 1989 has taught photography at the Academy of Fine Arts in Ravenna. Guidi has participated in numerous exhibitions. He has published a number of monographs and is the subject of many articles and texts.

JEAN GUIMARÃES

Guimarães was born in 1955 in Rio de Janeiro where he currently lives and works. He graduated with a doctorate degree in biophysics from the University of Rio de Janeiro. Guimarães received the Marc Ferrez Prize, Rio de Janeiro in 1988. He has exhibited his work at Parque Lage, Rio de Janeiro; Casa Triángulo, São Paulo; and the Rotterdam Biennal in 1990.

DEBORAH HAMMOND

Hammond has shown work at numerous venues, including the Corcoran Gallery of Art, Washington, D.C.; International Festival of Women Photographers, London; Photo Metro Gallery, San Francisco; and Mois de la Photographie, Paris. She is represented in a number of public collections, such as the Center for Creative Photography, Tucson, Arizona; the Museum of Photography, Tel-Hai, Israel; and the Gernsheim Collection at the Harry Ransom Humanities Research Center at the University of Texas at Austin. Hammond is the subject of a number of articles in publications such as *Artweek*, *Photo Metro Magazine*, *World of Photography*, and *Photo Review*. She has won the Marin Arts Council Visual Arts Fellowship (1994) and the Ruttenberg Foundation Award (1997).

TRACY ANNE HART

Hart's credits include portraits of Stevie Ray and Jimmie Vaughan, Joe Ely, and Buddy Guy in *Guitar World*, *Guitar Player*, *Musician*, *People*, *Japanese Guitar Player*, the *Austin Chronicle*, and the *New York Times*. Her work has been broadcast on Epic/Sony home video, VH-1 *Legends*, and PBS. Hart has shown her work in several exhibitions, including the Texas Photographic Society's Governor's Exhibitions and FotoFest, as well as in auctions for Houston radio station KLOL. She is represented in Houston by the Heights Gallery, which she has co-owned since 1984.

LINDA HAYWARD

A native of Montreal, Canada, Hayward received her B.F.A. in photography from Concordia University. She is currently completing her M.F.A. at the University of Houston. She works with original and borrowed photographic, print images and text, sometimes presenting them in mixed-media sculpture settings. Her work has been exhibited in Montreal at the VAV gallery, in Toronto at the Canadian Broadcasting Corporation, and in various group shows in Houston.

JOHN HERRIN

Born in 1940, Herrin currently resides in Houston. He pursued journalistic-style photography in high school and college; however, he is substantially a self-taught artist. After college, photography was a relatively dormant part of his life until 1986, when he purchased a large-format camera and his work became more abstract and conceptual. Recently, Herrin has begun exploring digital processing in order to produce color pigment prints. His work has been included in several exhibitions and is in the collection of the Museum of Fine Arts, Houston, as well as various corporate and private collections.

KAI-OLAF HESSE

Born in 1966 in Lower Saxony, Germany, Hesse studied communications design at the University of Essen and photography with Professor Joachim Brohm at the University of Leipzig, Germany. After spending three years on the book project *Bauhaus Dessau—Industrielles Gartenreich* at the Bauhaus in Dessau, Germany, he spent the last two and a half years photographing in the United States. Hesse has participated in Focus '96 in Dortmund and in *Kuntpreis Landkreis* in Gifhorn, as well as in other recent exhibitions in Berlin, Bilderbad, Cologne, Herten, and Munich. He has published work in *Contemporary German Photography*.

ED HILL AND SUZANNE BLOOM (MANUAL)

Since 1985 Bloom and Hill have been working in digital media, manipulating photographs, and creating installations and interactive computer programs for museums and galleries. They contemplate the vicissitudes of nature and cyberculture in their electronic studios in Vermont and in Texas, where both have been professors of art at the University of Houston for twenty-one years. Their work has been exhibited widely throughout this country and abroad and is included in the collections of the Museum of Contemporary Photography, the Los Angeles County Museum of Art, and the International Museum of Photography, among others. Their current projects include producing electronic art for a new wastewater testing facility being built by the City of Houston, maintaining a Web site for digital imaging, and developing an eccentric approach to the pastoral landscape.

JANE HINTON

Born in Victoria, British Columbia, Canada, Hinton now lives and works in Toronto, Ontario. She studied at St. Martins School of Art in London and Ontario College of Art in Toronto. She has been represented by Inman Gallery since 1990, and is also represented by Mira Godard Gallery in Toronto. Hinton's recent two-person show, *Dark Bridges: Mackenzie/Hinton*, was on view at Kitchener-Waterloo Art Gallery in Kitchener, Ontario and traveled to Gallery Lambton in Sarnia, Ontario. The show was documented by a catalogue with an essay by artist and guest curator Tony Urquhart. In 1997 Hinton's work was featured in *New Work: Gallery Artists* at Inman Gallery in Houston and in *Spring Sampler: Three Houston Galleries* at Transco Tower Gallery in Houston, which was curated by Sally Sprout. Her work is part of the permanent collection of the Museum of Fine Arts, Houston.

GEORGE HIXSON

Hixson's black-and-white photographs have been shown at DiverseWorks Artspace, the Contemporary Arts Museum, and other Houston venues. His work, most recently was part of the Lesikar Gallery show titled *Jesus and Elvis: Two Kings*. Hixson attended the University of Bridgeport in Connecticut, but moved to Houston in the early 1980s. He has been published in the *New York Times*, the *Washington Post*, and the *San Francisco Bay Guardian*. His work is part of numerous private collections. Hixson resides in Houston.

CLAUDIA JAGUARIBE

Born in 1955 in Rio de Janeiro, Jaguaribe received a Bachelor's degree in art history from Boston University in 1979. Since 1989 she has lived and worked in São Paulo as an independent photographer, specializing in advertising, fashion, and journalism. Jaguaribe has had solo exhibitions at Escola de Artes Visuais, Rio de Janeiro, 1985; Curitiba Photography Week, 1991; and Galería Fotoptica, São Paulo, 1993. Her work has been included in group exhibitions in Rio de Janeiro, São Paulo, and Paris.

CHAD JOINER

A graduate of the Milwaukee Institute of Art and Design (B.F.A., 1995), Joiner is currently a graduate candidate at Tufts University/School of the Museum of Fine Arts, Boston. His work discusses masculinity and the role it plays in the development of the adolescent male.

CARLOS JURADO

Born in 1927 in Chiapas, Mexico, Jurado received his formal artistic education at the Esmeralda school of the Escuela Nacional de Artes Plásticas in Mexico City. As a painter and photographer, he has participated in over thirty exhibits, more than thirteen of which have been as solo artist, including a 1986 retrospective of his work at the Museum del Chopo in Mexico City. In his career, Jurado has founded the college of art at the Universidad Veracruzana, established a system of art courses for the public, and developed the Alternative Technology school dedicated to the use of inexpensive but high-quality materials throughout the artistic process. He has gained critical acclaim from art critics and won several national and international awards, including a lifelong achievement prize given by the government of his home state, Chiapas.

TIMOTHY PAYNE KARR

Karr received his B.F.A. in photography from Cornish College for the Visual and Performing Arts in 1989. Since moving from New York to Hanoi in 1993, he has worked as a photojournalist for the Associated Press, the *New York Times*, and Agence France Presse. Karr was the *Asiaweek* correspondent for Vietnam from 1993 to 1995. He helped establish the *Vietnam Investment Review*, that country's most influential English-language newspaper, where he has served as managing editor from 1993 to 1997. His photographs have been published in major magazines and journals throughout the world, including *ArtForum*, the *International Herald Tribune*, and *Le Monde*. Karr has shown work in group exhibitions throughout the United States and has recently returned to the United States to print images from over four years in Hanoi. He currently lives in Boston.

WILLIAM KENTRIDGE

Kentridge was born in 1955 in Johannesburg, South Africa. Since 1980, he has worked in various media—drawing, film, and theater. During this period, he has participated in fourteen solo exhibitions and numerous group, exhibitions including *Art from South Africa* at the Museum of Modern Art in Oxford and *Memory and Geography* at *Africus*, the First Johannesburg Biennale. Kentridge has won numerous prizes and awards, including the Standard Bank Young Artist award in 1987 and the Blue Ribbon award at the American Film Festival in New York. He recently participated in the *Sixth Biennale* in Cuba, *Dokumenta 1997* in Germany, and exhibited an installation piece at *SITE Santa Fe* in New Mexico.

JENNIE KING

Born in 1973 in Columbus, Ohio, King moved to Houston in 1992 to attend Rice University and continues to live and work in Houston. Trained as an art historian, she recently served as visual arts coordinator at DiverseWorks Artspace and currently teaches art history at Houston's High School for the Performing and Visual Arts.

ROBO KOCAN

Born in 1968 in Poprad, Slovakia, Kocan has shown his work in group exhibitions such as *Images of Europe*, Amsterdam; *Slovaks in Dijon*, Dijon, France; *Profiles 94-International*, Skoki, Poland; and *Schattenwerfer*, *Forum schloss Wolkersdorf*, Austria. He has also shown work in solo exhibitions, including the *Month of Photography* in Bratislava, Slovakia, and has won awards in the exhibition *Image of Europe* in 1992 and 1995.

CLARE LA GROUE

La Groue is a self-taught photographer who has never missed an Art Car Parade along the streets of Houston. She has shown her work locally and has recently become the proprietor of her own photography studio in downtown Houston. She enjoys listening to the beat of her own drum, even when it is a little out of sync. La Groue resides in Houston.

AN-MY LÊ

Lê received an M.F.A. in photography from Yale University in 1993. In her career, she has worked as a researcher in immunology and coauthored various papers in that field; as a staff photographer for the Compagnons du Devoir, a guild of French artisans; and as a teaching assistant and lecturer at the university level. Lê currently works as a freelance photographer and computer graphist. She has participated in a number of exhibitions and has won several grants and awards, including the John Simon Guggenheim Memorial Foundation fellowship in 1997. Lê is represented in the collections of the Museum of Fine Arts, Houston, the Museum of Modern Art in San Francisco, and the Bibliothèque Nationale in Paris.

VIVIAN LEE

Born in 1971 in Seoul, Korea. Lee came to America at age nine with her family. She has lived in Houston since then and considers Houston her hometown. The project of photographing the downtown Houston area has great importance to her. By working with the downtown and its community, Lee was able to express her appreciation for the city that brought her to America. Her first contact with photography was in a photojournalism class in high school. She continued to develop her photographic study and skills at the Glassell School of Art, the Art Institute of Houston and the University of Houston. She is currently working on her B.A. in journalism with a minor in political science at the University of Houston. Lee has also been working as a freelance photographer for the *Houston Chronicle* "This Week" for seven years. Although her daily work revolves around photojournalism, her personal photography mixes her passion for photography with political issues.

DAVID LEVINTHAL

Levinthal, who lives and works in New York City, has won grants from the Guggenheim Foundation and the National Endowment for the Arts, as well as the Polaroid Corporation Artist Support Grant. He has had many solo exhibitions, including shows at the International Center for Photography, New York; Philadelphia Museum of Judaica; Modern Art Museum of Fort Worth, Texas; Bibliothèque Nationale, Paris; Wiener Staatsoper, Vienna; and Museum Für Gestaltung, Zurich. Levinthal's work is in many collections, including the Art Institute of Chicago, the Brooklyn Museum, the Museum of Modern Art, New York, the Museum of Fine Arts, Houston, and the Whitney Museum of American Art, New York.

RUTH LIFSCHITS

Born in 1944 in Rio de Janeiro where she currently lives and works, Lifschits earned a degree in industrial design at the Federal University of Rio de Janeiro and studied photography in Brazil and the United States. She has taught photography at the School of Visual Arts in Rio since 1992. Lifschits had a solo exhibition at the Funarte Gallery, Rio de Janeiro in 1995. Her work has beeen included in group exhibitions such as *Recent Photographic Art from Brazil*, Photographer's Gallery, London, 1996 and *Brazil of the Brazilians*, Kunsthaus Zurich, 1994.

JAVIER RAMÍREZ LIMÓN

Born in 1960 in Hermosillo, Sonora, Mexico, Limón studied photography in Mexico and New York. From 1989 to 1996, he taught audiovisual techniques, the Zone system, and alternative methods in palladium printing at Escuela Activa de Fotografia in Mexico City. He has participated in a number of solo and group exhibitions throughout Mexico. Limón's series *Reconstrucción de Familia* (fifteen photographs) was selected for *Muestra Lationamericana de Fotografía 1996* by Centro de la Imagen for the Latin American colloquium at *Fotoseptiembre 96* in Mexico City.

LUCÍA MINDLIN LOEB

Born in 1973 in São Paulo where she currently lives and works, Loeb utilizes photography as a means of self-expression. She exhibited at the *International Month of Photography* in São Paulo in 1993 and has had her work included in group exhibitions at the Center for the Arts at Yerba Buena Gardens, San Francisco, 1994, and Centro Cultural Banco do Brasil, Rio de Janeiro, 1995.

TSUGUMI MAKI

Maki lives and works in Boston. She received her B.S. from Ithaca College and was a 1996 American Photography Institute National Graduate Seminar Fellow at NYU. She is currently completing her M.F.A. degree at Tufts University/School of the Museum of Fine Arts, Boston. Her current work documents the characteristics of memory and attempts to explore the condition of memory, as well as to bring consciousness to the eclectic collections of the mind.

RUBENS MANO

Born in 1960 in São Paulo where he currently lives and works, Mano holds a degree in architecture. He organizes exhibitions and workshops with photographers in São Paulo and has had a solo exhibition at Galería Fotoptica, São Paulo in 1988. Mano's work has been included in group exhibitions at MoMA São Paulo, 1990, and June Festival, 1993.

STEPHEN MARC

Marc currently resides in Chicago. He earned an M.F.A. in photography from the Tyler School of Art, Temple University in Philadelphia in 1978. Marc is a full-time faculty member of the Columbia College photography department (Chicago) as well as the coordinator of the graduate program in that department. He is the recipient of many grants and awards, including a visual arts fellowship in photography from the National Endowment for the Arts and an Aaron Siskind Foundation fellowship from the School of Visual Arts in New York. Marc has participated in numerous solo and group exhibitions. He self-published the book *Urban Options*, Ataraxia Press. His work appears in the book *The Black Trans-Atlantic Experience*, University of Illinois Press, as well as in a number of journals, periodicals, and magazines. Marc is represented in a number of public collections.

SHIRLI MARCANTEL

Born in Texas, Marcantel lives and works in Houston as a designer of gardens and horticultural consultant. She has studied photography at the University of Houston, the Rice Media Center, and currently at the Glassell School of Art. Marcantel has exhibited with the Texas Photographic Society and the Mexic-Arte Museum in Austin, the Galveston Arts Center, and the Rice Media Center in Houston. Her work is in the photography collection of the Museum of Fine Arts, Houston and numerous private collections.

FRANK MARTIN

Born in 1942 in New Orleans, Martin died prematurely in 1994. After a brief stay at Louisiana State University in the mid-1960s, he made his living as a professional photographer. Martin's work began to mature and take shape in the late 1980s and he achieved recognition in both solo and group exhibitions. In addition to his powerful, ethereal, and abstracted images of cities and nature, Martin was a beloved photographer of impromptu gatherings of the Houston arts community. He is represented in numerous private and public collections, including the Menil Collection, Houston; the Museum of Fine Arts, Houston; the City of Houston, Office of the Mayor; the Center for Creative Photography, Tucson; and the Art Institute of Chicago among others.

KAGISO PAT MAUTLOA

Mautloa was born in 1952 in Ventersdorp, Western Transvaal, South Africa. Between 1966 and 1973, he studied art in Soweto, Johannesburg, and Rorkes Drift, Natal. He won the O.K. Young Graphic Designer award in 1980. Mautloa has been a voluntary teacher at FUBA, Mofolo Art Center, and a graphic designer for S.A. Broadcasting Corporation. He has participated in a number of exhibitions, including a solo show at the National Art Museum in Botswana, *GRAFOLIES '93* at the *Abidjan First Biennal* in the Ivory Coast, and *Vita Art Now*, which traveled from the Johannesburg Art Gallery to the *Venice Biennal* in Italy.

ANNE ARDEN MCDONALD

Born in London in 1966, McDonald received her B.A. with Honors in art from Wesleyan University, Middletown, Connecticut in 1988. Her work has been exhibited in solo and group exhibitions, including *The Will of the Wisp*, Atlanta Gallery, Atlanta, Georgia; *Personal Rituals*, American Culture Center, Prague, Czech Republic; *International Fototage*, Herten, Germany; and Spazi, Politecnico, Rome, Italy. McDonald's work is represented in many collections and is the subject of a number of published articles and catalogues. She has received commissions for work on album covers, posters, and book covers, among other projects. McDonald won a Savannah College of Art and Design Scholarship for Summer Art Study in London and Paris (1984) and was included in the *Who's Who of American Women* (1996).

AMANDA MEANS

Means currently resides in New York City. This spring she will have a solo exhibition of recent work at Ricco Maresca Gallery in Chelsea. Her floral studies are photograms in which she uses actual flowers and leaves as negatives in the enlarger. The work is distinguished by the richness of the black-and-white tones resulting from this process. Means is a printer and teacher and has been featured in many solo exhibitions and collections. Her work has been shown in the Avon Collection at the International Center for Photography; the National Museum of Photography, Film and Television in Bradford, England; the National Gallery of Canada in Ottawa; and the Claes Nordenhake Collection in Stockholm.

JOSÉ MEDEIROS

Born in 1921 in Teresina, Piaui, Brazi, Medeiros is considered one of the most important Brazilian photojournalists. He began as an amateur in Teresina and is currently a freelance photographer for Tabu and Rio magazines. He photographed for the *O Cruzeiro* magazine throughout its halcyon days until 1962. In 1965, Medeiros focused his interests on films as director of photography, working with the best Brazilian film directors. His publications include *Candomblé*, 1957, and *José Medeiros—50 Years of Photography*, published by Funarte, Rio de Janeiro, 1986.

KATE MELLOR

A landscape photographer, Mellor is based in Hebden Bridge in the South Pennines, England. After graduating with a degree in photography from Manchester Polytechnic Faculty of Art & Design, she joined the artists' collective the Albert Street Workshop. She has exhibited her work widely in Britain and has authored *Unnatural History*, *Island: The Sea Front*, and *Blue Shift.*. Mellor has received commissions titled Regeneration and Wasteland, both from Site Gallery (formerly Untitled), Sheffield; Landscapes from Tasmania for Leeds General Infirmary; and *Spa: In the Steps of Robert Pinnacle* for the Mercer Art Gallery, Harrogate, in conjuction with *Photo 98*, the *European Festival of Photography and the Electronic Image*. In 1994, Mellor won the Yorkshire and Humberside Major Award for Photography Production. She is currently a part-time lecturer in photography at Cumbria College of Art.

DANIEL MENDOZA

Born in 1957 in Mexico City, Mendoza studied photography at the Facultad de Artes Plásticas at the Universidad Veracruzana. From 1983 to 1986 he studied under Nacho López, and in 1987 Mendoza founded Imagenjarocha, the first photo agency in the state of Veracruz. He was department head of Plastic Arts at la Universidad Veracruzana. Mendoza has participated in over thrity group exhibitions and has published work in national and international magazines and periodicals. He has worked as a photographer for the photo agency imagenlatina and currently is a photographer for the newspaper *El Economista* in Mexico City.

BILLIE MERCER

Mercer resides in Houston, Texas and works primarily in black-and-white photography. She recently has begun to explore work with hand-coated, light-sensitive processes such as argyrotype. For more than three years she has worked on an extensive project in Mexico, photographing sixteenth-century churches for which she received a fellowship from the Houston Center for Photography. Mercer has been in several one-person shows and in numerous competitions and invitational exhibitions. Her work was recognized in 1995 with an Honorable Mention by the Texas Governor's Show in San Antonio, juried by Ann Tucker, photography curator at the Museum of Fine Arts, Houston. Mercer's work is included in the Photographic Correspondence Collection of that museum and in a number of private collections.

ARTHUR MEYERSON

A native Texan, Meyerson travels extensively throughout the world photographing for corporate, advertising, and editorial assignments. He is included in the World's Top Ten Annual Report Photographers listing by *Communication World* and has been named *Adweek* Southwest Photographer of the Year on three occasions. Recently, *American Photo Magazine* named Meyerson as one of the top thirty advertising photographers. His photographs have been exhibited internationally and have been featured in many publications, including *Communication Arts*, *Photo Pro*, *Photo Design*, *Zoom* (France), *Rangefinder*, *Portfolio*, *Idea* (Japan), *Novum* (Germany) and *Photo World* (China).

WILL MICHELS

Michels received a Bachelor of Architecture degree with Honors from Pratt Institute, Brooklyn. Currently his photography deals primarily with self-portraits, addressing issues of privacy and identity. His work has been shown in a number of curated and juried exhibitions in the Houston area. He was recently awarded a 1997 grant from the Cultural Arts Council of Houston to photograph veterans of the battleship U.S.S. Texas. His work will be in the exhibition *The Self-Portrait* in Switzerland in the fall of 1997. Michels' work is represented in numerous collections, including the Museum of Fine Arts, Houston. Lives in Houston.

GERARDO MONTIEL KLINT

Born in 1968 in Mexico City, Mexico, Montiel earned his Bachelor's degree in industrial design (1994) and is currently a Master's candidate in architecture at the Universidad Nacional Autónoma de Mexico, Mexico City. He has participated in two solo exhibitions as well as a number of group exhibitions throughout Mexico. Montiel has published work in magazines and is represented in the public collections of Centro de Arte Moderno in Guadalajara and Centro Integral de Fotografía, Puebla, Mexico. He is a member of the Consejo Mexicano de Fotografía in Mexico City.

ZWELETHU MTHETHWA

Born in 1960 in Durban, KwaZulu Natal, South Africa, Mthethwa earned his M.F.A. in imaging art at the Rochester Institute of Technology. In his career, he has held positions such as cultural organizer for the Department of Education and Training and lecturer of photography and drawing at Michaelis School of Fine Art at U.C.T., among others. In 1987 Mthethwa won a Fulbright scholarship to study in the United States. He has participated in numerous exhibitions, including the Memorial Art Museum in Rochester, New York; *Grand Prix International d'Arts Plastiques* in L'Aigle de Nice; and a group show at the National Museum of Contemporary Art in Olso, Norway.

MARIO CRAVO NETO

Born in 1947 in Salvador, Bahia, Brazil, where he currently lives and works, Cravo Neto is considered one of the most prestigious Brazilian photographers. He studied photography and sculpture at the Art Student's League in New York in 1969-70. Cravo Neto has had solo exhibitions throughout Brazil, Europe, North America, and Japan, including *FotoFest '92* in Houston. He has widely exhibited in group shows in Brazil, at five editions of the *São Paulo Biennal*, and in Zurich, Paris, Milan, New York, Arles, Copenhagen, and many other cities. Cravo Neto has published five books. He is represented by Witkin Gallery, New York and Fahey/Klein Gallery, Los Angeles.

EUSTÁQUIO NEVES

Neves lives in Belo Horizonte, Brazil. He has shown work in a number of solo and group exhibitions, including *Man, Industry, and Environment* at the *24th Winter Festival* at the University of Minas Gerais, Brazil; *Fotofagia*, FUNARTE, Rio de Janeiro; *The Individual and Memory*, Havana; and the *IIith Biennial of Tokyo*, Metropolitan Museum of Photography. Neves has published work in several catalogues and magazines, including *Novas Travessias: Contemporary Brazilian Photography*, edited by VERSO/Maria Luiza Melo, Carvalho/London; *Eustáquio Neves Monograph*, edited by Autograph/London; *ZAPP—Electronic Magazine*, Belo Horizonte; and *LUNA CÓRNEA*, Mexico.

HILDEGART MORENO OLOARTE

Born in 1973 in Veracruz, Mexico, Oloarte is currently enrolled as an undergraduate student in photography at the Universidad Veracruzana in Xalapa, Veracruz. She has participated in a number of solo and group exhibitions and has published her work in various national and international catalogues and magazines. In 1996, Oloarte won first prize at the *Segundo Salón de la Fotografía* at the Centro de Arte Moderno in Guadalajara and earned an Honorable Mention at the *Eighth Biennial of Photography*, Mexico in 1997.

KENJI OTA

Born in 1952 in São Paulo, where he currently lives and works, Ota received a Bachelor's degree in political science from the São Paulo School of Sociology. Ota was awarded the Incentive Prize by the government of São Paulo in 1993. His interest lies in technical and aesthetic research with unconventional applications. Ota's work has been included in the *17th São Paulo Biennal*, 1983; *Brazil Projects*, the Institute for Art and Urban Resources, New York, 1988; and the *International Photography Month*, São Paulo, 1993.

PHILIPPE PACHE

Born in 1961 in Lausanne, Switzerland, Pache has exhibited widely throughout Switzerland in both solo and group exhibitions. His work is represented in a number of public collections and has been the subject of many articles. He has won several first prize awards, including First Prize at Grand Prix Suisse de la Photographie, Zurich. Pache is represented by Galerie Bodo Nemann, Berlin and Galerie Camera Obscura, Paris.

WARREN PADULA

Born in 1947, Padula currently lives in Sag Harbor, New York. He studied architecture with Louis Kahn and has a degree in sculpture. After exhibiting sculpture for twenty years, Padula began showing photographs in 1990. His work was selected for the *Discoveries of the Meeting Place* at FotoFest '96 in Houston, and he has had solo shows at Blue Sky Gallery, Portland, Oregon; Rathbone Gallery, Albany, New York; Houston Center for Photography; and Photo Metro Gallery, San Francisco. He has exhibited in numerous group shows, including the Musée de la Photographie, Charleroi, Belgium and the Print Club, Philadelphia.

PAVEL PECHA

Born in 1962 in Kremnica, Slovakia, Pecha studied photography in Prague. His group exhibitions include *Nine-Speed Cloudy Bicycle*, Trnava, Slovakia; *Contemporary Slovak Photography*, Stockholm, Sweden; *Between Image and Vision*, Scotland, Romania, Germany, and Slovenia; and *Le Corps*, Mulhouse, France. His solo exhibitions include *My Intuitive Theatre* in Slovakia and Austria; *Dream Fields*, Slovakia and Italy; and *Photographies*, Slovakia.

GEORGE PETERS

Born in 1949 in Chicago, Peters escaped from Art Center School in Los Angeles in 1972. Over the last twenty-eight years, Peters has been a sidewalk portrait artist, an animated film artist, graphic artist, architectural model maker, environmental sculptor, installation sculptor, kite maker, world traveler, writer, performance artist, puppet maker, theater set designer, costume maker, and aerial sculptor. In 1982 he relocated to Boulder, Colorado where he currently lives. He has collaborated with Melanie Walker on installations and commissions for the past three years.

PATRICK PHIPPS

Phipps is editor and producer of *Trick Hips*.

SEAN POREA

Born in 1961 in Newport, Rhode Island, Porea enrolled at East Texas State University in Commerce in 1979 and received his Bachelor of Science degree in photography. After graduation, he went to work in a commercial studio in Houston. After six years, Porea freelanced as a photographer and also worked as a photographic lab manager. In the summer of 1992, he enrolled at Sam Houston State University to earn his Master of Arts degree in photography. Following the completion of his degree, Porea worked full-time as a commercial photographer and part-time as photography instructor at North Harris Montgomery Community College. He is currently working on his figure studies using black-and-white infrared materials.

RUDO PREKOP

Born in 1959 in Kosice, Slovakia, Prekop graduated from the Film and Television Faculty Academy of Performing Arts in Prague in 1986. He now lives and works as a freelance photographer. In 1991 he coauthored the scenario and the creative design of Warhol's Family Modern Art Museum in Medzilaborce, Slovakia. Prekop has participated in approximately seventy-five group exhibitions at home and abroad. He is represented in numerous public and private collections.

VICKI RAGAN
Ragan received an M.F.A. degree in photography and printmaking from the University of Arizona in Tucson in 1981. She has shown work in exhibitions, including *Perception: Field of View*, Los Angeles Center for Photographic Studies; *Recent Acquisitions*, Brooklyn Museum of Fine Art; and *Enthusiasm Strengthens*, Center for Creative Photography at the University of Arizona. Ragan received a commission for a permanent installation at the Hartfield International airport in Atlanta in celebration of the 1996 Summer Olympic Games. She has published work in two books, *The Edible Alphabet Book*, Bulfinch Press, Boston (1995), and *Oaxacan Wood Carving: The Magic in the Trees*, Chronicle Books, San Francisco (1993).

ROGERIO REIS
Born in 1954 in Rio de Janeiro, where he currently lives and works, Reis earned a degree in journalism from the Universidade Gama Filho in 1978. He was a member of Agência F4 from 1985 to 1987 and a cofounder of Agência Tyba, with which he is still involved, in 1989. Reis was editor of photography with the newspaper *Jornal do Brazil* from 1991 to 1995. He has had solo exhibitions at Centro Cultural in Curitiba and Centro Cultural Light in Rio de Janeiro. His work has been included in group exhibitions in Rio de Janeiro, 1983; the *2nd Biennal of Photography* in Rotterdam, 1990; in Zurich, 1992; and in *Casa de América* in Madrid, 1994.

ROSÂNGELA RENNÓ
Born in 1962 in Belo Horizonte, Rennó currently lives and works in Rio de Janeiro. She earned a degree in architecture and visual arts at the University of Minas Gerais in 1987. In 1994 Rennó received a Master's degree at Escola Guignard and a Master's degree in arts and communications at the University of São Paulo. She was awarded the Marc Ferrez Photography Prize in Rio de Janeiro in 1992. Rennó has widely exhibited her work in solo and group shows in Brazil and abroad, including the National Museum of Woman in the Arts in Washington, D.C., 1993, *Aperto, Venice Biennal*, 1993; and the *V Bienal de la Habana*, 1994.

MAURICE ROBERTS
Born in Houston, Roberts has produced and performed in several multimedia installations, including *Symphony of Idols* at DiverseWorks Artspace in Houston, which focused on photography and music created in Central American war zones. His photographs of art cars have been widely exhibited and have also been used to decorate a section of Texas Children's Hospital. Roberts is the editor of *Art Cars: Revolutionary Movement*, produced by Ineri Publishing, where he is now chief of operations. Roberts resides in Houston.

ORVILLE ROBERTSON
Born in 1957 in Jamaica, Robertson has exhibited his work in many solo and group exhibitions and is represented in public collections such as the California Museum of Photography; the Bibliothèque Nationale, Paris; the Schomburg Center for Research in Black Culture, New York; and the Center for Creative Photography, Tucson, Arizona, as well as in private collections. He has published work in various journals and newspapers. Robertson is publisher and editor of *Fotophile*, a photography journal, and a contributing editor of *Rfinder*, a California-based photography journal.

ABBY ROBINSON
Robinson has participated in a number of solo and group exhibitions, including *Autoworks*, the Workshop in Hong Kong; *Women Artists Series*, Rutgers University in New Brunswick, New Jersey; and shows at the International Center of Photography in New York and the Creative Photography Gallery in Cambridge, Massachusetts. She has published work in the *New York Times*, *Newsday*, and *PHOTO*, and in the books *Women See Me*, McGraw-Hill Co.; *Ornamentalism*, Clarkson N. Potter, Inc.; and *Women Photograph Men*, William Morrow and Co.

SEBASTIÁN RODRÍGUEZ ROMO
Rodriguez was born in 1973 in Mexico City. He has studied the arts in Italy and Mexico, where he studied with Diego Toledo, José Miguel González Casanova, and Jesse Lerner. Rodriguez has participated in two solo exhibitions as well as the group exhibitions *Lentes para la Abstracción*, Casa de la Cultura de Coyacan, and *Instalación de Fin de Siglo y Milenio*, X-Teresa, Centro Hispánico in Mexico City.

SANDRA R. RUDY
A documentary, fine art, and travel photographer, Rudy earned a Bachelor of Arts degree (1964) and a Master of Arts degree (1967) at Baylor University. She completed her postgraduate study at St. John's College in Santa Fe, New Mexico in 1968 and has attended numerous photography workshops. Rudy has traveled extensively and has exhibited her photography in collaboration with Steven Jay Rudy. She is represented in numerous public and private collections. Rudy is a member of the Royal Photograph Society in Bath, England and has been on the board of directors of the Center for the Arts, Crested Butte, Colorado; the Santa Fe Festival of the Arts Foundation; and the Main Street Art Happening, Houston.

STEVEN JAY RUDY
Born in Houston, Texas in 1945, Rudy is a documentary, fine art, and travel photographer. He has traveled extensively, both as an American serviceman and as a photographer. Through his background in architecture and sculpture, he has won awards and produced commissioned works as well as participated in exhibitions. He has exhibited his photographic work in collaboration with Sandra R. Rudy and is represented in numerous public and private collections. Rudy is a member of the Royal Photograph Society in Bath, England and has been on the board of directors of Crested Butte Society, Colorado; the Center for the Arts, Crested Butte, Colorado; the Santa Fe Festival of the Arts Foundation; and the Main Street Art Happening, Houston.

DEBRA RUEB
Rueb resides in the Texas bay area, where she teaches and works as a photographer. She has a B.A. in photography from Sam Houston State University and an M.F.A. from the University of Houston. A founding member of the Houston Center for Photography, Rueb has exhibited in group and solo exhibitions and has been published in a variety of magazines. Her work is a personal exploration of the familiar, such as her family, women's issues, and a children's series.

SEBASTIÃO SALGADO
Born in 1944 in Aimorés, Minas Gerais, Brazil, Salgado has lived and worked in Paris since 1973. He is one of the leading photojournalists in twentieth-century photography. He was awarded the Eugene Smith Award, 1982; the Eastman Kodak and Paris Audiovisual, 1984; the World Press in Holland, 1985; the Journalism Prize, I.C.P. in New York, 1986; the Photographer of the Year, American Society of Magazine Photography; the Erich Salomon Prize in Germany, 1988; the King of Spain Prize, 1988; the Victor Hasselblad Prize in Sweden, 1989; and the Great Prize of the City of Paris, 1991. He was elected honorary member of the American Academy of Arts and Sciences in 1991. Salgado has exhibited worldwide.

PENTTI SAMMALLAHTI
Sammallahti was born in 1950 in Helsinki, Finland. He began to photograph in 1961 and soon joined the Camera Club in Helsinki, where he met the photographers Antero Takala and Jussi Aalto, among others. Sammallahti has traveled throughout Europe, Morocco, Turkey, and Asia and has produced many portfolios and books reflecting his expeditions. After seventeen years of teaching at the University of Art and Design, he won a prestigious fifteen-year state artist grant in 1991. He has won several prizes and awards, including the Finnish Critics Association Annual Prize in 1980 and State Prizes for Photography in 1975, 1979, and 1992. His work is represented in numerous collections, including the Parliament of Finland; the Bibliothèque Nationale, Paris; and the Museum of Modern Art, New York. Sammallahti is well-known for his book designs and innovative printing techniques.

EDWARD SHAW
Born in New York, Shaw moved to Buenos Aires in 1960, where he is an art critic, collector, travel writer, and photographer. Over the past fifteen years, his work has been exhibited in various institutions in Argentina and Spain. Most of it is dedicated to chronicling political and cultural phenomena.

TOMAS SHAW
Shaw is twenty-one years old and currently lives in Buenos Aires, where he photographs the urban scene. He traveled with his father, Edward, to the twenty-five towns included in *Saving Salamone* and took most of the photographs in the exhibition.

JEFF SHORE
Born in 1969 in Richmond, Indiana, Shore has lived in Houston since 1979, where he currently lives and works. He received a B.F.A. in painting and drawing from the University of North Texas, Denton in 1991. Previously focusing on painting, his recent body of work has become more three-dimensional, including interactive components. Shore has participated in numerous group exhibitions throughout Texas. A one-person exhibition, *A Room With a View*, is scheduled for Lawndale Art and Performance Center, Houston, in 1998.

PENELOPE SIOPIS
Born in 1953 in Vryburg, South Africa, Siopis received a B.F.A. (1974) and an M.F.A. (1976) from Rhodes University and completed a postgraduate course in painting at Portsmouth Polytechnic in England. She has exhibited in eight solo and numerous group exhibitions in South Africa, Europe, and the United States. Siopis has participated in a number of conferences and has been the subject of published articles in texts and journals, including *The Baby and the Bathwater: Motif, Medium, and Meaning in the Work of Penelope Siopis*, written by E. Rankin. She is represented in several public collections and her work has been featured in numerous television documentaries.

PEDRO SLIM
Born in 1950 in Beirut, Lebanon, Slim earned a Bachelor's degree in architecture at the Universidad Anahuac in Mexico. He studied photography at Escuela Activa de Fotografía at El Centro Cultural de Arte Contemporáneo with Ralph Gibson, Greg Gorman, James Luciana, Brian Young, Laura Cohen, and Gerardo Suter. Slim has participated in five group exhibitions, as well as in his solo exhibition *De la Calle al Estudio* at the Museo del Chopo. His work was selected for Mexico's *Seventh Biennial of Photography* and he was one of three award winners at the *Eighth Biennial of Photography*.

L'UBO STACHO
Stacho was born in 1953 in Handolova, Czechoslovakia. He studied at the Slovak Technical University and the Academy of Fine Arts (FAMU). Stacho has shown work in numerous solo and group exhibitions in Europe, Canada, and the United States, including *FotoFest 88*, Houston; Malra de Villennes-sur-Seine, France; *Fotografía Txecoslovaca Contemporánia*, Cercle Cultural de la Fundació "La Caixca", Barcelona; and *Mail Art Projekt*, Musea Internationale de Neu Art, Vancouver. He has curated several exhibitions and has given a number of lectures, including *Slovak Contemporary Art*, Rochester Institute of Technology; *About Communication*, Dubrovnik; and *Slovak Contemporary Art*, Tyler School of Art, Temple University in Philadelphia.

VASIL STANKO
Born in 1962 in Myjava, Slovakia, Stanko studied photography in Prague. He has participated in numerous group exhibitions, including *Festival Torino Fotografia*, Turin, Italy; *Foto Festival*, Amsterdam; *Vision del homme*, France; and *Internationale photographie*, Czech Republic. Stanko has shown work in solo exhibitions at Galerie Fotochema, Prague; Kulturelle Zentrum der CSFR, Berlin; Galerie Profil, Slovenia; and Galerie Pecka, Prague. He is represented in a number of collections and is the author of numerous articles.

WILL STONE
Born in the northeastern United States, Stone resides in Webster, Texas. He photographs landscapes in black and white, with a surreal, impressionistic style. With his mother, a botanist, he published a book, *The Great Public Gardens of the Eastern United States*. His work has been seen in numerous solo and juried exhibitions and is represented in collections, including that of the Harry Ransom Humanities Research Center, University of Texas; the Museum of South Texas, Corpus Christi; and the Santa Barbara Museum of Art, California.

MIRO SVOLÍK
Born in 1960, Svolik studied photography at the School of Applied Arts in Bratislava, Slovakia and received a degree from the Department of Photography at the Film and Television Faculty Academy of Performing Arts in Prague in 1987. He has published work in *Revue fotografie*, *ART News*, *European Photography*, and other journals. Svolik has won the Infinity Award and the Young Photographer Award of the International Center of Photography, New York. He also works in the design of record covers, book illustrations, and other publications.

PHILIP TAPLIN
Currently residing in Washington, D.C., Taplin works with color photography, video, and multimedia focusing on iconic cultural landscapes. He recently completed a solo show, *AmerIcons*, at Gallery K in Washington, D.C. His photographs are included in private and corporate collections. He has exhibited in numerous group shows and has received regional and national awards. Taplin was the first recipient of a Master's degree in photojournalism from the University of Minnesota. He received advanced training at the Maine Photographic Workshops, the Anderson Ranch Arts Center, and the Woodstock Photography Workshops.

FANNIE TAPPER
Tapper resides in Houston, Texas and has worked full-time in photography since 1988. Her portrait-tableaux reflect her doctoral thesis on poetic narrative (Ph.D., French literature, Rice University). She has fourteen solo shows to her credit, including those at the Houston Center for Photography, 1993; Galveston Arts Center, 1994; Women & Their Work, Austin, 1996; Museum of Southeast Texas, Beaumont, 1998; and Lynn Goode Gallery, 1993, 1994, 1996, 1998. Tapper's work is included in numerous private, corporate, and museum collections.

IRVING TEPPER
Born in 1947 and a native of St. Louis, Missouri, Tepper now lives in Manhattan. For three decades his art has been featured in exhibitions such as Gallery Paule Anglim in San Francisco, Newport Harbor Art Museum, the Kunstmuseum in Bern, Switzerland, and the St. Louis Museum of Art. His work has been published internationally and is represented in museum collections around the world, including the Museum of Contemporary Art in Los Angeles, the Victoria and Albert Museum in London, the San Francisco Museum of Modern Art, the Kunstmuseum in Bern, and the St. Louis Museum of Art. Tepper has taught courses in several disciplines at the Rhode Island School of Design, the San Francisco Art Institute, the University of California, Berkeley, and New York University, among others.

EVIN THAYER
Thayer earned a Bachelor of Arts degree in communication from the University of Houston, where he studied theater. He credits the now-retired professor Cecil Pickett with encouraging him to search for and accept nothing less than perfection in his artistic endeavors. Thayer's current work, *The Evin Thayer Celebrity Series*, focuses on his recognition of outstanding native and adopted Houstonians and their contributions as politicians, humanitarians, entrepreneurs, medical or science pioneers, philanthropists, sports personalities, or entertainers. His photographs have appeared in publications such as *Houston Metropolitan*, *Texas Monthly*, *DBA*, *Houston Health and Fitness*, *L'Ink*, *Texas Woman*, *Inside Houston*, and the *Media Ink Publications*. Thayer has been featured in the *Professional Photographers of America* magazine and has been a guest lecturer on fashion photography at *FotoFest '94* in Houston.

DANNY TISDALE
Tisdale earned his M.F.A. degree at Otis/Parsons School of Design in Los Angeles in 1985. He has shown work in numerous solo and group exhibitions, as well as performances and projects such as *Flux-Attitudes: Transitions, Inc.*, the New Museum of Contemporary Art, New York; *Danny Tisdale: An Artist for a Change*, Interactive Campaign Headquarters installation at the Upper Albany Neighborhood Collaborative with Real Art Ways, Connecticut; and *Auto-Portrait: The Calligraphy of Power*, Exit Art/The First World, New York. Tisdale has won many grants and awards, including the Franklin Furnace Performance grant in 1993 and a National Endowment for the Arts fellowship in 1995. He is the subject of numerous published articles in *Artforum*, *Black Popular Culture*, the *Los Angeles Times*, and the *Village Voice*.

KAMIL VARGA
Born in 1962 in Stúrovo, Slovakia, Varga is a freelance photographer who currently lives and works in Prague. He studied photography at the Secondary School of Applied Arts and at the Academy of Film, TV, and Photography in Prague. Varga has participated in approximately forty group exhibitions at home and abroad, including Norway, Poland, Russia, Switzerland, Germany, and the United States. He is represented in a number of public collections, including Musée de l'Elyseé, Lausanne, Switzerland; Recontres d'Arlés, France; and Landenshaus, Germany, as well as in private collections.

CASSIO VASCONCELLOS

Born in 1965 in São Paulo, where he currently lives and works, Vasconcellos has worked as a freelance photographer since 1981 and lately specializes in publicity. His solo exhibitions include *Small Portraits of Augusta Street*, Museu de Arte de São Paulo, 1982; Casa de las Américas, Havana, 1985; and *FotoEspacio*, Buenos Aires, 1987. Vasconcellos' work has been shown in group exhibitions at Mois de la Photo, Paris, 1986; Milan; Stedelijk Museum, Amsterdam; Lisbon, 1989; *Rencontres d'Arles*, 1991; *FotoFest '92* in Houston; and various shows in Brazil.

ADRIENE VENINGER

Born in 1958 in Slovakia, Veninger immigrated with her family to Canada, where she studied fine art and design and currently lives and works. She has exhibited work in both solo and group exhibitions and is represented in a number of collections. Veninger is the subject of a number of articles in journals such as *American Photo*, *Photo Magazine*, and the *British Journal of Photography*. She has produced several book covers. In 1997 she was awarded the Protégé Honour by the Arts Foundation of Greater Toronto.

TERRY VINE

Born and raised in a small town in northeast Ohio, Vine currently lives and works in Houston, where he has been shooting commercially for over twelve years. While his corporate and advertising work has taken him around the world and won many prestigious industry awards, Vine's personal work centers on black-and-white studies of the cities and rural areas of Europe. His work has been featured in many solo and group exhibitions and is in the collection of the Museum of Fine Arts, Houston as well as numerous private collections.

BOB WADE

Wade was born in 1943 in Austin, Texas, where he currently lives. He received a B.F.A. from the University of Texas, Austin and an M.A. from the University of California, Berkeley. Wade is the recipient of three National Endowment for the Arts awards. His work has been exhibited in biennials in Paris, New Orleans, and the Whitney Museum of American Art, New York. Wade is represented in the collections of Chase Manhattan Bank, AT&T, and the Menil Collection. He has produced three books, and is currently showing work in the traveling exhibition *New Realities—Hand Colored Photographs* 1839 to the Present.

MELANIE WALKER

Born in 1949 in Glendale, California into a family in which photography was the primary passion and topic of discussion. Walker received an B.F.A. from San Francisco State University. She studied with Robert Fichter at Florida State University and received an M.F.A. in 1974. Walker has received an Aaron Siskind Foundation grant and a National Endowment for the Arts photography fellowship. As an image-maker, she works not only with photography, but also with fabric, sculpture, puppetry, sound, theater, performance, and costumes. Walker relocated to Boulder, Colorado in 1992 to teach at the University of Colorado. She began collaborating with George Peters in 1995.

FREDERIC WEBER

Born in 1955 in New York City, Weber received a B.F.A. in film from New York University in 1977. He taught basic black-and-white photography at a Sarah Lawrence College course in France in 1982. Weber received a fellowship from Art Matters, Inc. and is represented in collections such as the Denver Art Museum; the George Eastman House, International Museum of Photography, Rochester, New York; the Museum of Fine Arts, Houston; and the Whitney Museum of American Art, New York.

DANIEL WEINSTOCK ARENOVITZ

Born in 1957, Weinstock has participated in a number of solo and group exhibitions in Mexico, Spain, and the United States. He has worked as a staff photographer in Mexico for Centro de Experimentación Teatral and in the United States for Bilingual Foundation of the Arts, Los Angeles and Compañia de Repertorio Español, New York. Weinstock has worked as a freelance photographer for several magazines and newspapers, including *Spy Magazine*, the *New York Times*, *Tiempo Libre*, *Hoy*, and *América Economía*.

SUE WILLIAMSON

Williamson was born in 1941 in England. Her family immigrated to South Africa in 1948 and she later earned an advanced diploma in fine art at the Michaelis School of Fine Art in Cape Town. Besides using prints as a medium, Williamson also produces site-specific installations using materials such as laser prints, steel, fabric, resin, and found objects. She often incorporates sound and lighting effects. Williamson has participated in a number of solo and group exhibitions. Her work appears in the books *Art in South Africa: The Future Present* and *Resistance Art in South Africa*, both published by David Phillip Publishers in Cape Town and St. Martins Press in New York. She is represented in several public collections.

BILL WILLIS

Willis is a visual artist primarily interested in printed matter, images of popular culture, and the folly of painting. He lives and works in Houston with his wife, Maggie.

DAVE WILSON

Born in 1946 in Tucson, Arizona, Wilson lives with his wife in Houston and works in Angola, West Africa for an international oil tool company. Self-taught in photography, he began his work with travel photography and documentation of the streets and older neighborhoods in Houston. In 1991 he was sent by his company to work with the fire-fighting effort in Kuwait. Wilson assisted Jean Caslin in organizing *The Scorched Earth: Oil Well Fires in Kuwait*, an exhibition at the Houston Center for Photography. He has also shown this work in several Texas venues. Wilson's current project deals with documentation of public art and informal portraiture.

BILL WITTLIFF

Born in Taft, Texas, Wittliff currently resides in Austin. His documentary project *Vaquero: Genesis of the Texas Cowboy* (1969-71) has been exhibited in numerous galleries and institutions in the United States and Mexico. He has done many screenplays as well as motion picture and television productions, including *Lonesome Dove*. Wittliff has founded two prestigious collections: the Wittliff Gallery of Southwestern & Mexican Photography and The Southwestern Writers Collection, both at Southwest Texas State University in San Marcos.

MARIANA YAMPOLSKY

Born in Chicago, Yampolsky has been a Mexican national since the 1940s. She is one of the best known photographers in Mexico, and her prints and photographs have been exhibited internationally. Yampolsky is represented in major collections, including the Museum of Modern Art, New York and the Wittliff Gallery of Southwestern & Mexican Photography in San Marcos, Texas. She is also known worldwide as a curator and educator and has been involved in many publications of her own work and the work of others. She will have a major retrospective at Centro de la Imagen in Mexico City this year.

FRANK YAMRUS

Yamrus earned a B.S. degree at Wilkes University, Wilkes-Barre, Pennsylvania (1980) and an M.B.A. degree at Drexel University, Philadelphia (1986). He has exhibited his work widely throughout the United States in both solo and group exhibitions. Yamrus has published work in numerous journals and is represented in public collections. He has won a number of awards, including from the Society of Contemporary Photography, Kansas City; California Discovery Awards; and the New Mexico Photography Competition.

PETER ZUPNÍK

Born in 1961 in Levoca, Slovakia, Zupník currently lives and works in Paris and Prague. He studied photography at the Secondary School of Applied Arts and at the Academy of Film, TV, and Photography in Prague. He has shown work in solo exhibitions including Galéria FOTO, Poland; Galerie Gijzenrool, the Nertherlands; Galerie Le Pont Neuf, France; and Institute Français, Prague. Zupník has participated in approximately forty group exhibitions at home and abroad.

CURATORS

FREDERICK BALDWIN

A founder of FotoFest in 1984, Baldwin was a photographer for many years. He worked around the world and his photographs were published in *Esquire, National Geographic, Life,* the *New York Times, Newsweek, Geo* and many other national and international publications. Baldwin taught photography at the University of Texas at Austin and the University of Houston, Central Campus. He was Peace Corps director in Borneo in the 1960s. Baldwin's book, We Ain't What We Used to Be (date?), documents the Civil Rights Movement in Georgia. He is coauthor of the book *Coming to Terms, the German Hill Country of Texas* (1991). Baldwin has been president of FotoFest since 1984. His work is represented in many public collections, including the Bibliothèque Nationale in Paris, the Museum of Fine Arts, Houston, and the Harry Ransom Humanities Research Center at the University of Texas at Austin.

DIANE BARBER

Barber is based in Houston. She has worked as curatorial assistant at the Houston Center for Photography and, from 1991 to 1997, for FotoFest, where she served as exhibitions and publications assistant and then as coordinator. Barber has recently assumed the position of visual arts coordinator for DiverseWorks Artspace in Houston. She is an active member of the Houston Coalition for the Visual Arts, having cochaired Houston's 1997 observance of World AIDS Day. Barber is currently working with photographer Nancy McGirr to organize a traveling exhibition of work from *Out of the Dump,* a project established to teach documentary photography to children in Guatemala City.

LUCIA BENICKÁ

Born in 1963 in Slovakia, Benická received her Magister of Arts degree at the University of J. A. Komensky in 1987. Her extensive experience in the arts extends to her roles as curator, art manager, lecturer, writer, and exhibits organizer. She has been involved in a number of exhibitions, including *Alexander Jirousek: Photographs, Young Slovak Photographers/Generations '60,* and *Communications.* Benická is the director of the House of Photography in Poprad, Slovakia, and she recently received a Fulbright Fellowship for photographic research in Chicago. She is the author of numerous articles and texts in publication and has also contributed her expertise to the production of documentary films.

JOHANNES BIRRINGER

Born in Germany, Birringer has resided in Houston since 1987 and works internationally as an independent choreographer and video artist. In 1993, after directing his first large-scale multimedia theater productions in Houston, Birringer founded AlienNation Co. and produced a series of workshops and cross-cultural collaborations in the U.S., Europe, and Latin America, including a performance/digital art project (LBLM) and several new dance/film concerts (*Lovers Fragments, Before Night Falls,* and *Between the Places*). His film, *La Lógica que se Cumple,* was premiered at the *Havana International Film Festival* and the *Chicago Latino Film Festival* in 1996-97. Birringer is currently building an electronic performance laboratory in Houston while continuing to collaborate with members of AlienNation Co. and independent artists, both locally and abroad. For the *FotoFest* project, he has invited as guests choreographer Sandra Organ, theater artist Gabriela Villegas, singer/composer Lourdes Pérez, and filmmaker Chan Uk Park.

MARCEL BLOUIN

Blouin received a B.S. from Montreal University and a Master's in art history from the Université du Quebec in Montreal. He is a founding member of Vox Populi, a center for the diffusion and production of photography, and of *Mois de la Photo à Montréal,* a biennial photo festival. Blouin is also the editor of the photo magazine *CVPhoto.*

ANA CASAS BRODA

Casas was born in 1965 in Granada, Spain. She studied art at the Universidad Autónoma de México and photography at the Escuela Activa de Fotografía and Casa de las Imágenes before earning her bachelor's degree in history at the Escuela Nacional de Antropología e Historia. Casas worked as assistant to Manuel Alvarez Bravo in 1985 and since then has worked as a freelance photographer. Since 1994 she has served as coordinator of workshops at the Centro de la Imagen in Mexico City. Casas has shown work in numerous solo and group exhibitions and has also published work in books, catalogues, and magazines, including *La Fotografía* (Spain), *Photographos Magazine* (Greece), and *Azteca México: Las Culturas del México Antiguo* (Lugwig Editores, Madrid, 1992).

FERNANDO CASTRO

Castro was born in 1952 in Lima, Peru. He attended high school in New York and later returned to Peru for pre-medical studies at the Universidad Peruana Cayetano Heredía (1972-75). Castro then switched careers and studied philosophy at that institution and at Rice University under a Fulbright fellowship (1979-85). His interest in the interaction of text and image began early and in 1983 he published the book *Five Rolls of Plus-X,* based on an earlier 1977 work of the same name. He has also authored *Martín Chambi, de Coaza al MoMA* (1989). Castro has been a photography critic since 1989 and is a regular contributor to Spot, *Art-Nexus* (Colombia), *Cámara Extra* (Venezuela), and *Taxi* (Peru), among others. He has curated many exhibitions, including *Modernity in the Southern Andes: Peruvian Photography 1900-1930* (1992), *The Broken Vessel* (1993), *O espelho oscuro* (1995), *Wisdom of Pain* (1996), and *Traces of Glass* (1998). Castro currently lives in Houston and is curator of photography at the Sicardi-Sanders Gallery.

ROLAND CHARLES

A photojournalist and the director of Black Gallery, a Los Angeles exhibition space, Charles actively promotes fine art photography. He has distinguished himself through his own work, which appears in books, in national publications, and on album covers, and through his continuing support of the arts. Charles is a founder and director of Black Photographers of California and a founding board member of the Jazz Photographers Association and Photo/Friends of the Los Angeles Public Library. He serves on the board of the Museum of African-American Art and the Los Angeles Center for the Photographic Studies. For Eastman Kodak, Charles was the associate producer and host of the television documentary *The Legacy Continues: California Black Photographers.* He is curator and one of ten photographers in the one-hundred-print exhibition *Life in a Day of Black L. A. : The Way I See It* and coeditor of the 148-page book of the same name.

JOHN CLEARY

Cleary has been a private collector for the past twenty years and a fine art photography dealer for the last six years. He is a member of the Houston Art Dealers Association and is also on the advisory board of the Houston Center for Photography. Cleary travels worldwide to attend auctions and exhibitions dealing with fine art photography. Recently, he opened the John Cleary Gallery in Houston, which features black-and-white photography.

MIGUEL FEMATT ENRÍQUEZ

Born in 1949 in Mexico City, Fematt studied the creative production of radio and television. He later studied visual arts at the Universidad Nacional Autónoma de Mexico. Fematt has participated in over twenty solo exhibitions throughout Mexico and in over fifty group exhibitions both nationally and internationally. He has published photographic work, as well as essays and reviews, in newspapers and magazines both nationally and internationally. A founding member of Foto-Apertura, Fematt is a council member of the Galería del Estado in Xalapa, Veracruz. Since 1982 he has served as chairman of the photography department at the Universidad Veracruzana and from 1991 to 1996 he was the general secretary of the faculty of plastic arts at that institution. Fematt has served as speaker at the *Coloquio Universitario de Fotografía de la UNAM Azcapotzalco* in 1994, 1995, and 1997, as well as portfolio reviewer at *FotoFest 96* and the *Fifth Colloquium of Latin American Photography,* Mexico City in 1996. He is represented in many private collections.

MARÍA TERESA GARCÍA PEDROCHE

García Pedroche received an M.F.A. from Texas Woman's University in Denton, Texas. She is associate curator at the Meadows Museum, Southern Methodist University in Dallas. García Pedroche directs and develops education and public programs, including special exhibitions, and has taught at various colleges in the Metroplex and curated and co-curated several exhibitions of Latino and Dallas artists. She was awarded a grant to serve as instructor and director of Art as a Universal Language/Art as Culture, providing art workshops for children as part of the Neighborhood Touring Program, funded by the Cultural Affairs Commission of Dallas (1990-95).

LINDA GIVON

Givon is one of the most respected and influential gallery owners in the world. She graduated with a B.A. degree from the University of the Witwatersrand and studied drama at the London School of Drama before pursuing a life-long career in art. Givon joined the Grosvenor Gallery in London in 1964, where she did extensive research on and promotion of dissident Soviet artists. During her career, Givon has promoted and introduced well known international artists such as Vikto Vasarely and Yvaral. She has contributed her expertise to the Department of Arts and Culture (DAC) since 1990, culminating in the South African participation in the *Fifth Biennial of Havana*. Givon is active in the work of community art centers and has recently relocated her gallery, Goodman Gallery to more spacious quarters, where she plans to pursue art consultancy.

JOSHUA GREENE

Greene began his career in photography by apprenticing for his father, Milton H. Greene. At age thirteen he was working in the darkroom at his father's studio. Greene went on to print, edit, and do post-production work as manager of their New York studio. His photographic interests lie in people, home furnishings, and food. During the mid 1970s he produced the first of many cookbooks with Lee Bailey, including *Country Weekends*, *City Foods*, and *Country Desserts*. Greene has committed himself for a three-year period to the restoration and marketing of his father's 300,000-image collection and has created a new company, the Archives of Milton H. Greene, L.L.C. He has mastered the art of digital photography in order to help restore many of his father's color images, which time has deteriorated and faded.

ANDY GRUNDBERG

Director of the Friends of Photography in San Francisco, Grundberg is a highly regarded writer, lecturer, curator, and teacher in the field of photography. He was educated at Cornell University and at the University of North Carolina at Greensboro, where he received an M.F.A. Formerly the photography critic for the *New York Times*, he is the author of *Crisis of the Real*, a collection of critical essays; *Alexey Brodovitch*, *Photography and Art: Interactions since 1946* (with Kathleen McCarthy Gauss); and *Mike and Doug Starn*.

SUNIL GUPTA

Born in India, Gupta is a Canadian citizen who lives and works in London as a photographer, curator, and editor. In 1983, he graduated from the Royal College of Art in London and became involved with the development of Black Arts in Britain. He is a founder of Autograph: The Association of Black Photographers in London. Gupta's works have been seen at the Havana Biennale (1994) and his most recent solo show was at Focal Point Gallery, Southend, Essex (1995-96). He has organized several exhibitions and edited accompanying books, including Disrupted Borders, Ecstatic Antibodies: Resisting the AIDS Mythology. Since 1993, Gupta has worked as curator for the Organisation for Visual Arts Limited (OVA).

MARTINO MARANGONI

Born in 1950 in Florence, Italy, Marangoni moved to New York in 1972 to study photography at the Pratt Institute. After returning to Florence, he taught photography at the Studio Arts Centers International and later founded the Studio Marangoni, a center for contemporary photography providing training courses and exhibition space. In his work, Marangoni combines photographic research with teaching. He is active both in his Florence studio and in other centers throughout Europe and the United States. Marangoni has participated in a number of solo and group exhibitions and is represented in several public collections.

CATHERINE McINTOSH

McIntosh began her career in 1977 with the *Claremont Courier* in California, a small-town paper known for its innovative use of photojournalism. She is photo editor for the features department at the *Houston Chronicle* and art director of that newspaper's Sunday *Texas Magazine*. McIntosh's fast-paced job involves planning assignments and selecting photographs for a wide variety of subjects, from fashion and food illustrations to documentary picture stories. Previously, she was art director for *Houston City Magazine* and *Houston Home and Garden Magazine*.

PATRICIA MENDOZA

Mendoza studied art history at the Universidad Ibero-americana in Mexico City and has broad experience in the plastic arts. She is a founding member of the Mexican Photography Council, coordinator of the Contemporary Art Forum, and director of Los Talleres Gallery. Mendoza coordinated the second *Latin American Colloquium of Photography* and the *Art and Identity Latin American Colloquium*. At the National Council for Culture and Art, she has been executive coordinator of the following projects: *Ciudad de Mexico 20s-50s*; *Museums: Where Knowledge Is Shared*; *Ecos y Reflejos*; and *Fotoseptiembre*, a month of photography in Mexico City. She is the author of numerous magazine and newspaper articles and critical essays on photography. Mendoza is currently director of the Centro de la Imagen.

JOSÉ IGNACIO ROCA

Roca currently resides in Santafé de Bogotá D.C., where he is an architect and museographer. He has lectured on museography and museums throughout Colombia and abroad. As chief of visual arts for the Luis Ángel Arango Library in Bogotá, he has organized several exhibitions on photography. For the planned expansion of the Luis Ángel Arango Cultural Complex, Roca has designed a gallery especially devoted to photography.

JOSÉ ANTONIO RODRÍGUEZ

Resides in Mexico City. From 1983 to 1986, Rodríguez founded and directed the Archivo Historico y Fotografico in Tabasco, Mexico. From 1989 to 1994, he served as curator and deputy director of the Museo Estudio Diego Rivera. Since 1994, he has worked as an independent curator, organizing exhibits for the Museum of Modern Art and the Franz Mayer Museum in Mexico City, among others. His published books and catalogues include *Manuel Alvárez Bravo, los años decisivos: 1925-1945 (1992)* and *Edward Weston: La mirada de la ruptura (1993)*.

OSVALDO SÁNCHEZ

Sánchez was born in 1958 in Havana, Cuba and has resided in Mexico since 1990. From 1984 to 1990, he was professor at the Academia San Alejandro and at the Instituto Superior de Arte of La Havana. Sánchez was formerly assistant director of plastic arts for the *Festival Internacional Cervantino*. He has published essays and articles on Latin American art in *Third Text*, *ArtNexus/Arte* (Colombia), *Poliéster*, and *Arte Internacional*, among other publications. In 1995 Sánchez received a grant from the Fondo Nacional para la Cultura y las Artes de México for his work as an art critic. He has curated and/or coordinated exhibitions featuring artists such as Robert Mapplethorpe, Joan Miró, Pablo Vargas-Lugo, and Diego Toledo, among others.

WENDY WATRISS

A founder of FotoFest in 1984, Watriss has worked as a newspaper reporter, producer of television documentaries, and freelance photographer. Her photo-documentary essays have been published in national and international publications such as *Stern*, *Life*, *Geo*, the *Smithsonian* magazine, *Newsweek*, the *New York Times*, and many others. Watriss is the recipient of many awards, such as the World Press Photo, Oskar Barnack Award, and Mid-Atlantic Arts Alliance/National Endowment for the Arts Award, among others. She is coauthor of *Coming to Terms*, the *German Hill Country of Texas* (1991) and editor of *Image and Memory*, *Photography from Latin America 1865-1994* (1998). Watriss has been artistic director of FotoFest since 1991.

ADAM WEINBERG

Weinberg earned an undergraduate degree from Brandeis University and a Master's degree from the Visual Studies Workshop/SUNY Buffalo. He has been curator of the permanent collection at the Whitney Museum of American Art since 1993. At the Whitney, he curated and co-curated numerous exhibitions, including *Hopper in Paris*; *Isamu Noguchi: Early Abstraction*; *In a Classical Vein: Works from the Permanent Collection*; and *Picassoid*. Weinberg has held posts as the artistic director at the American Center in Paris, director of the Equitable Center Branch of the Whitney Museum, and chairman of the NEA Museum Panel. He has also served as a panelist for the Seattle Arts Commission, the Minnesota State Arts Board, the Massachusetts Council on the Arts, and the Canadian Cultural Center, among others.

ACKNOWLEDGMENTS

EXHIBITIONS

Marcus Adams, *Commerce Street Art Warehouse, Houston*

Andrew Albers, *Houston*

Enrique Arce, *Salón de Fotografía, Guadalajara, Mexico*

Association Française d'Action Artistique, *Ministry of Foreign Affairs, Paris*

Diane Auberger, *Magnum Photos, Paris*

Michelle Barnes, *Community Artists Collective, Houston*

Linda Haag Carter, *Art League of Houston*

Fernando Castro, *Houston*

Jennifer Childress, *One Allen Center, Houston*

Kimberly Davenport, *Rice University Art Gallery, Houston*

Robyn Finke, *Houston*

Leah Freid, *Lombard/Freid Gallery, New York City*

Lubicka Ftorekova, *House of Photography, Poprad, Slovakia*

Greg Garrett, *Winter Street Art Center, Houston*

Linda Givon, *Goodman Gallery, Johannesburg, South Africa*

Mike Golden, *Houston Community College Art Department, Houston*

Deborah Grotfeldt, *Project Row Houses, Houston*

Sharon Haynes, *Solero, Houston*

Robo Kocan, *Slovakia*

Jane Lombard, *Lombard/Freid Gallery, New York City*

Rick Lowe, *Project Row Houses, Houston*

Wendy Luers, *The Foundation for a Civil Society*

Frédéric Marsal, *Paris*

Jamie Mize, *Treebeard's, Houston*

Roy Murray, *Wagon Works Building, Houston*

Dr. Miroslav Musil, *Embassy of Slovakia, Washington D.C.*

Patricia Mendoza, *Centro de la Imagen, Mexico City*

Jean Luc Monterosso, *Maison Européene de la Photographie and Mois de la Photo, Paris*

Arturo Sánchez, *Mexico City*

Marcos Santilli, *NAFOTO, Sao Paulo, Brazil*

Jorge Salas, *Consul General of Peru, Houston*

Harvey Seigle, *Winter Street Art Center, Houston*

María Inéz Sicardi and Jim Sanders, *Sicardi-Sanders Gallery, Houston*

Harvey Seigle, *Winter Street Art Center, Houston*

Chuck Spahr, *Vine Street Sudios, Houston*

Sally Sprout, *Transco Tower and Sally Sprout Gallery, Houston*

Jack and Stephanie Stenner, *Purse Building Studios, Houston*

Lily Sverner, *NAFOTO, São Paulo, Brazil*

Dan Tidwell, *Treebeard's, Houston*

David Thomas, *Indochina Arts Project, Boston*

Fletcher Thorne-Thomsen, Jr., *Vine Street Studios, Houston*

Emily Todd, *DiverseWorks ArtSpace*

Pampa Risso-Patrón, *Pan American Foundation, Houston*

John Tsertos, *QRT Management, Houston*

Eugenio Valdés Figueroa, *Havana, Cuba*

Kathy Vargas, *Guadalupe Cultural Arts Center, San Antonio*

Cinda Ward, *Palace Cafe and Hogg Grill, Houston*

Michael Winhof, *Houston*

Geoff Winningham, *Rice Media Center, Houston*

Nancy Worthington, *Nancy Worthington Fine Art, Houston*

FESTIVAL

Andrew Albers, *Houston*

Jackie Alfred, *Theater District Association*

Johannes Birringer, *AlienNation, Houston*

Jody Blazek, *Houston,*

Nancy Brainerd, *Downtown Houston Association*

Marsha and Jack Carter, *Houston*

Mary Kay and Bob Casey, *Houston*

Gary Coover, *Greater Houston Preservation Alliance*

Blake Cordish, *The Cordish Company, Baltimore*

Roy and Mary Cullen, *Houston*

Jessica Cusick, *Cultural Arts Council of Houston/Harris County*

Romona Davis, *Greater Houston Preservation Alliance*

Jeff DeBevec, *Houston*

Christian Escudié, *Air France*

Bob Eury, *Downtown District*

Steve Filippo, *Market Square Historic District*

Kimberly Gremillion, *Gremillion & Co. Fine Art Inc.*

Guy Hagstette, *Downtown Houston*

Patricia and Lucas Johnson, *Houston*

Jim and Sherry Kempner, *Houston*

James Kiely, *Houston*

Keith Krumweide, *School of Architecture, Rice University*

Diann Lewter, *Downtown District*

Victoria and Marshall Lightman, *Houston*

Jim Maxwell, *Market Square Historic District*

Gerald Moorhead, *Houston*

Alphons Mueggler, *Consul General of Switzerland, Houston*

Dung Ngo, *School of Architecture, Rice University*

Pete Radowick, *Houston Convention & Entertainment Facilities Department*

Ashley Smith, *Downtown District*

Richard Stout, *Houston*

Linda Sylvan, *Rice Design Alliance*

Paul Tetreault, *Alley Theatre*

G.J. "Jordy" Tollett, *Convention & Entertainment Facilities Department and Greater Houston Convention and Visitors Bureau*

Dede Whitehurst, *Wyndnam Warwick*

Geoff Winningham, *Rice Media Center*

Harold Wolpert, *Alley Theatre*

SPECIAL

Toni Beauchamps, *Houston*

Barry Engel, *Vinson and Elkins, Houston*

Bruce Rieser, *British Airways*

William Steen, *Menil Collection, Houston*

Muffy Stout, *Washington D.C.*

Paul Winkler, *Menil Collection, Houston*

Harry Zuber, *Legg, Mason, Wood, Walker, Houston*

VOLUNTEERS

Beverly Barrett

Laura Celle

Kathi Crum

Beth Daniel

Jeanne Dear

Rhonda Enck

Mercedes Gonzalez

June Lien

David Martinez

Ruben Martinez

Kendall McCarley

Alexandra Montgomery

Jonathan Mova

Philippe Paravicini

Doug Parker

Katie Phillips

Christine Rosales

Sonya Sullivan

Karen Whitaker

Jason Whittington

Jennifer Williams

Sunshine Winters

SCHOOL TOURS/ CURRICULUM

Marcia Carter

Wendy Ramires

Ruth Teleki

AUCTION COMMITTEE

Karen Bering, *Fine Print Auction, Co-Chair*

Lisa Mathis, *Fine Print Auction, Co-Chair*

El Matha Wilder, *Auction Exhibition Chair*

Walter Bering

John and Martha Britton

Ashley Bryan

Beth Carls

Scott and Jennifer Clearman

Fulton Davenport

Laura Fain

Sue Finley

Sharon Froisey

Cab and Mary Gilbreath

Michael and Ceci Goldstone

Laffy and Joanie Herring
Pat Hogan
Rand and Lindsay Holstead
Karen Icenhower
Dan and Julie Japhet
Susan Japhet
Wendy Jones
Jenny Kempner
Don and Kay Kirby
Bobby and Alicia Kirkland
Inel Klein
Franny Koelsch
Courtney Lanier
Helen Leonard
Irene Liberatos
Amy Looper
Ransom and Isabel Lummis
Pam Marquis
Harry and Kathy Masterson
Will Mathis
Cece McCann
Terry Merwin
Kendall and Cindy Miller
Elizabeth Moore
Ellen Morris
Laura Morris
Charlie Neuhaus
Keith Nickerson
Stephanie Owens
Bonnie Rubey
Nancy Rust
Allison Sarofim
Christopher and Valerie
    Sarofim
Claire Squibb
Stan and Hillary Stratton
Jeff and Elizabeth Vallone

1998 MEETING PLACE VOLUNTEERS

Rabun Bistline
Walter Bistline, Jr.
CMS/Creative Marketing
Services
Carolyn Cullinan
Cia Devan

Linda Foot
Sharon C. Friesy
Carola Herrin
John Herrin
Bert Hungerford
Judy Hungerford
Leslie Carolyn Johnson
Judith Kaufman
Carolyn Keck
Connie Keck
Lida Keene
Nancy Laughbaum
Mickey Marvins
Mike McKann
Betty Mooney
Jake Mooney
Ken Parker
Nancy Parker
Jennifer Potter
Sandra Riley
Donna Rogers
June Russell
David Santonian
Mary Seriñá
Robert Silberg
Clarice Simpson
Bill Snypes
Amy Spangler
JoAnne White
Dave Wilson

MEETING PLACE REVIEWERS

Concepción Alarcón
Vince Aletti
M. Darcie Alexander
Don Bacigalupi
Fred Baldwin
Pavel Banka
Diane Barber
Vladimir Birgus
Suzanne Bloom & Ed Hill
    (MANUAL)
Pierre Blache
Chris Boot
María Teresa Boulton

Carol Brown
Lynne Brown
Peter Brown
Stephen Bulger
Jean Caslin
Fernando Castro
Fausto Chermont
John Cleary
Charlotte Cotton
Eric Davis
John Demos
Pierre Devin
Matthew Drutt
David Einsel
Kathleen Edwards
Miguel Fematt
Elizabeth Ferrer
Nancy Fewkes
Burt Finger
Roy Flukinger
Dana Friis-Hansen
Maria Teresa Garcia-Pedroche
Juan Alberto Gaviria
Alice Rose George
Sunil Gupta
Ellen Handy
Melissa Harris
Carroll (Ted) Hartwell
Robert Hebert
Lynn Herbert
Tom Hinson
Marita Holdaway
William M. Hunt
David L. Jacobs
Steven Kasher
Paul Kopeikin
Jo Leggett
Bruce Lineker
Celina Lunsford
Vaclav Macek
Angela Magalhaes
Martino Marangoni
Barbara McCandless
Catherine McIntosh
Patricia Mendoza
Joan Morgenstern

Stephen Morelock
Sarah Morthland
Andreas Müller-Pohle
Alison Devine Nordstrom
Stephen Perloff
Ron Platt
Chris Rauschenberg
Jane Levy Reed
Cheryl Reynolds
Carolyn Richards
José Ignacio Roca
Linda Rutenberg
María Inés Sanders
Martha Schneider
Mark Sealy
Miguel Seco
Karen Sinsheimer
Elizabeth Smith
Ann Stautberg
Carla Stellweg
Guy Swanson
Mary Virginia Swanson
Finn Thrane
Anne Tucker
Kathy Vargas
Georges Vercheval
Ricardo Viera
Keith Wallace
Jill Waterman
Wendy Watriss
Deborah Willis
Clint Willour
Geoff Winningham
Steve Yates

FotoFest is a nonprofit arts and education organization that promotes public appreciation for photographic art, international and cross-cultural exchange through photography and literacy through photography.